LEADERSHIP IN CHANGING TIMES

HOW ADAPTIVE LEADERSHIP IS REPLACING CLASSIC LEADERSHIP IN A POST-PANDEMIC WORLD

Tariq Khan

Kendall Hunt
publishing company

Cover image © Shutterstock.com

Kendall Hunt
publishing company

www.kendallhunt.com
Send all inquiries to:
4050 Westmark Drive
Dubuque, IA 52004-1840

ISBN: 978-1-7924-8193-2

Published in the United States of America

DEDICATION

Shamim N. D. Khan, my late mother and the reason of my being
N. D. Khan, my father, for teaching me survival
Khalid Jawed Khan, my brother, for being my inspiration
Anita, my wife, for being my unconditional support
Shan, my son, for teaching me tenacity
Alina, my daughter, for teaching me inclusiveness
Rayyan, my son, for giving me unending energy
My teachers, mentors, students, family, and GDM team, for all the continued learning

SPECIAL THANKS

To every person who rejected me and unintentionally gave me the fuel to carry on

TABLE OF CONTENTS

ABOUT THE AUTHOR

© T. Khan

Tariq Khan
Founder and CEO
Global Diversity Marketing
New York, New York
tkhan@gdmus.com

Tariq Khan is a global sought-after keynote speaker and a recognized business leader who brings the combination of corporate and professional leadership experience along with academic learning. His expertise includes thought leadership, innovative marketing strategy, cultural transformation, and the diversity and inclusion arena. He has had a distinguished twenty-year corporate career and has held senior leadership roles for major global Fortune companies, including ING, Nationwide, and MetLife. In his last corporate job, Tariq was Senior Vice President and Head of Market Development for ING.

In 2010, Tariq founded his company, Global Diversity Marketing (GDM) in New York. GDM is a leading management consulting firm that has helped global Fortune companies and coached C-Suites leaders to adopt and thrive in the changing environment. Tariq has equally impressive contributions in the nonprofit world. He serves on the board of directors/advisors for the APIA Scholars; the Asian Pacific Institute for Congressional Studies (APAICS); and Ascend, which is the largest Asian American professional network, and is president of OPEN Tri-State. He is also the chairman of the board of trustees at the Stratford University in Alexandria, Virginia.

Tariq especially enjoys his role as adjunct professor of marketing and leadership at New York University's SPS graduate school. Tariq has been a faculty member at NYU since 2005. Tariq earned a bachelor's degree in international marketing and advertising from Baruch College, New York; an MBA in marketing and management from St. John's University, New York; and an Executive Management Certification from Babson College, Massachusetts.

Tariq has spoken at major events around the world and shared stage with global CEOs, critical thinkers, and U.S. Presidents.

INTRODUCTION

WHY SHOULD ANYONE BE A LEADER?

Why not? Not everyone can be a leader, but you possibly can. Leadership is a responsibility, a liability, an asset, an honor, and an accomplishment. You can work hard and smart to make yourself a leader, but others have to accept you as a leader to lead effectively. Leadership is an art in theory and a science in practice. Leaders use scientific logic along with their emotional charisma to lead people.

Leadership is an activity that motivates people to act outside their comfort zone and follow or trust an individual (leader).

What motivates people to become leaders? Different leaders have different motives. A leader motivated by a cause may be quite different from a social media influencer. German Chancellor Angela Merkel has 1.8 million Instagram followers, compared to the 42.2 million Instagram followers and 169 million overall social media followers of seventeen-year-old Tik Tok sensation Charli D'Amelio. A few years ago, Angela Merkel closed her Facebook account, which had amassed 2.5 million followers, while Charli D'Amelio is always looking for every possible way to grow her social media following.

If a particular leader is not your type of leader but still has a huge following, then don't underestimate the power of that leader. Let people and history be the judge of who is a leader and who is not. Also, don't confuse *successful* leaders with *good* leaders. Some people might consider Adolf Hitler a successful leader, but history remembers him as a villainous. brutal dictator—not a good leader. Often, visionary leaders are ahead of their time and are not recognized for their skills until they are gone. Similarly, some leaders enjoy power and popularity, which are hyped far more than their accomplishments—and later on, history reveals their real stature.

I have been teaching leadership and marketing courses at New York University (NYU) graduate school since 2005. As an adjunct professor, I had a chance to read and use several books on leadership for my classes. There are some great books out there, but it seems that none of them address how leadership is evolving in response to changing times. At least, I haven't read them yet.

Classic leadership served organizations and leaders well in the past, but the pandemic in 2020 tested leaders like never before. It redefined many of the rules of engagement—as well as our audience and the products and services we offer, which have changed dramatically. In general, the old, classic engagement and leadership styles that were applicable in the past may no longer be relevant in their old style.

We must transform our leadership style from classic to adaptive if we are to thrive in the current environment of frenetic, forward-moving change.

When I was a student in school, my teachers always knew more than me because they spent years learning various subjects. Today, my students at NYU probably know more than I do, at least about some topics. Why? Because knowledge is so accessible. They know how to use technology better than I do. Although I consider myself pretty tech savvy, it was a shock for me when I would walk into classroom and say, for example, that Apple is worth a certain amount of money in terms of market valuation. Within seconds, my students would correct me and provide the exact amount of Apple's market valuation. Before I even finish asking a question, the students can come up with a detailed, correct answer.

So now, I am not only teaching while I'm in class but also learning from these incredibly bright young people. Although they might not have the insights I have, based on real-world experience, they are full of curiosity and have open minds. That is a great combination both for failure and innovation. Remember, today, failure is a requirement.

CHAPTER 1

How COVID-19 Has Impacted Leaders

CHAPTER LEARNING OBJECTIVES

1. Understand how to convert a challenge into an opportunity.
2. Identify leadership opportunity in your life.
3. Evaluate your surroundings to leverage the opportunity.

Have you read the introduction? If not, please go back and read it. You don't want to miss a good read. If you did read the introduction, I'm already liking you and see a great leadership potential.

The COVID-19 pandemic of 2020–21 reshaped the world in many ways. In fact, it will not be surprising if the world, for many years to come, refers to the time period before the pandemic as BC ("Before COVID-19"). COVID-19 challenged leaders like never before. This tumultuous and challenging time was a perfect test of leadership, and those who steered their teams and companies through this storm successfully have earned a virtual crisis-leadership badge.

Some people say that COVID-19 has taken us many years back. In my opinion, COVID-19 has taken us decades forward. The life we may not have envisioned for many years is here now. By far, COVID-19 has been a painful learning experience. It has taught us to be resilient, tenacious, patient, adaptive, and innovative. There will be a time when people will miss COVID-19 days, the family time, the laid-back life, the time to recalibrate. Of course, we will never forget the loss of invaluable people who untimely left us.

Once upon a time, people use to go to an outside workplace called an office, seriously! Talent that entered the workforce in 2020 may continue to work remotely for a few more years. At some point in time, they may have to go to work (an office outside their home) full time as some of us did our entire career. Imagine the HR challenges in bringing these people to a common work location that they are not used to? The leaders need to motivate people to come to work at an office. The leaders of yesteryears may have never thought of this as a challenge in the past. Don't be surprised if there is a mutiny from the younger workforce who do not want to go back to the office. In my opinion, the leaders have to provide a flexible workplace option if you want to retain the next generation's best talent. You can blame/credit COVID-19 for this work arrangement. I have been pleading for a four-day work week for a long time. It is time to do that now. Going forward, adaptability is going to be a key ingredient for the leadership to stay competitive and successful. The next challenge may come from an unknown and unexpected competitor/enemy. The next war may be fought in the cyber space through Artificial Intelligence (AI) which may be smarter than the Original Intelligence (OI). COVID-19 has made us more screen dependent, and we spend more time on our small screens. The six-hour outage of Facebook, Instagram, and WhatsApp in October 2021 supposedly caused $6 billion loss in net worth to Facebook CEO Mark Zuckerberg. Imagine if someone could hack the entire internet for a day what the cost would be for the world? Leaders, be prepared to fight new wars through new channels.

As a leader, you must hope for the best possible environment yet be prepared for the worst possible one. COVID-19 could possibly be a once-in-a-lifetime event, but then again, I stopped making predictions after seeing this unprecedented situation impacting not one country but the entire globe.

There are some success stories about leaders whose companies emerged from the pandemic stronger than before, but there are ample examples of failed leadership. I believe the world was unprepared for a challenge of this magnitude, which led to the loss of many lives and severe economic impact. Witnessing this leadership bankruptcy was an unpleasant surprise.

Where did we fail in terms of leadership? In my opinion, most of our leaders flunked in four tiers.

1. DENIAL

Many experts believe the COVID-19 virus originated in Wuhan, China, in December 2019. Unlike many other people, I learned about the severity of this virus immediately after it was known. I had quite a few Chinese students at New York University (NYU), and they all seemed to be quite concerned.

Living in New York, we didn't take it seriously until March 2020, although the first case in the United States was reported on January 21, 2020.[1] Across the globe, many denied that the virus was real. I remember attending Celine Dion concert in New York in March 2020 with no concern of the virus. This denial led, in part, to the demise of more than 4.5 million lives globally and counting.

2. ANGER

Once we realized that COVID-19 was not on a sojourn but rather here to stay, many immediately jumped to the anger stage, accompanied by the blame game. We saw no alignment among the local, national, and global leadership in terms of how to defeat the virus. These conflicting messages divided people rather than uniting them to fight a virus that was not willing to spare anyone. In leadership, this

1. "Timeline: How Coronavirus Got Started," Erin Schumaker, CNBC, September 22, 2020, https://abcnews.go.com/Health/timeline-coronavirus-started/story?id=69435165.

stage is among the most dangerous stages because even great leaders can make a wrong decision if they are blinded by anger.

The range of the anger was quite widespread; the prevailing feeling was, "We don't deserve this." Many people thought that 2020 was supposed to be the best year of their lives, but instead, the year led to large-scale cancellations or delays in vacations, graduations, promotions, reunions, surgeries, and many other events including many other life events. Everyone was angry at some point in time in 2020. How often do you see virtually everyone in the world angry at the same time? For many people, that anger will leave a long-term or permanent impact.

3. ADJUSTMENT

This is the most important stage, and it's where many leaders fail. Leaders' timing is always critical. Great leaders act at the right time. The leaders who proactively tackled the coronavirus did well in some cases but others waited too long to act. Their delayed decisions resulted in loss of human lives and the widespread economic shenanigans that came with the pandemic crisis. Many leaders were simply not prepared to overcome and adapt to the moving target of the virus. Good leaders got over the denial and anger phase quickly while accepting the changing work environment as the new normal.

As this book was being published, the aftermath of COVID-19 was still unfolding. No one knows how long it will take to realize the real damage the pandemic has done. However, like any other challenge, this situation also created opportunities for many. Bad leaders have perished, good leaders have survived, and great leaders have flourished.

4. DECISIVE AND EFFECTIVE LEADERSHIP

In any crisis, many people lose their footing, but a few emerge as victors. This was the case with COVID-19. We saw many leaders heed the call to adapt their processes and business models. They figured out ways to innovate in the face of the crisis instead of crumbling. This is the charge for every leader and entrepreneur: to exhibit decisive and effective leadership, *especially* during unprecedented times of crisis.

Due to the pandemic, many leaders retired early, many people became leaders earlier than planned, many leaders perished, and many new leaders emerged.

I WROTE THIS BOOK TO SIMPLIFY LEADERSHIP

I wrote this book to simplify leadership. I want to peel back the layers of the leadership "onion" and determine whether leadership in changing times is really complicated or if we are *making* it complicated.

This book is for anyone who is in a leadership position now or has an aspiration to lead. That includes young people who are entering the workforce, professionals who have been in the workforce for the past few years, and seasoned leaders who have led very well so far, but now, especially in the post-COVID-19 world and amid the changing rules of engagement, are encountering some anomalies in leadership that they have never seen before. Anyone who wants to be prepared for the changing work environment can benefit from reading this book.

I am sharing with you what I have learned, both as a leader in the corporate world and as an entrepreneur. I hope you can learn from the successes and failures I have experienced during my own journey and witnessed others doing. I thought about writing this book for a long time. It is my perspective on how leaders need to change to keep up with the frenetic pace of change that is occurring today.

We are living in a world in which people expect everything to be in an app, and they learn a lot of practical life lessons online.

As a parent, one of the most tear-jerking moments for me was when I walked into my son's room when he was a young teenager. He was sitting at his computer while tying a knot in his tie. I asked him, "What are you doing?"

He said, "I'm learning how to knot a tie."

I said, "I've waited all these years to teach you how to knot a tie."

He replied, "No, Dad. It's much simpler on YouTube."

Knowing everything about leadership won't necessarily make you a leader. How successfully you apply your knowledge will impact your success in your leadership journey.

MY JOLTING INTRODUCTION TO LEADERSHIP—BEFORE I BECAME A TEENAGER

As I was growing up in Pakistan with my family, the country was under martial law of a military dictatorship in the late 1970s. My family was active in politics. When I was twelve years old, both of my parents were arrested and put in jail because they were fighting for restoration of democracy against a military dictator, which was a serious offense. My parents were jailed or were kept under house arrest for most of the eleven years of dictatorship in Pakistan.

Pakistan was under martial law from 1977 until 1988. The Pakistan People's Party won the elections held on March 7, 1977, but the party's opponents, the Pakistan National Alliance, accused the Pakistan People's Party of rigging the elections. On March 14, 1977, the Alliance started a series of nationwide protests. New elections were announced for October 15, 1977, but on July 5, 1977, the Chief of Army Staff, General Muhammad Zia-ul-Haq, imposed martial law, and the elections were postponed. A conference of political leaders was held in February 1978, but a year later, in 1979, General Zia-ul-Haq declared political parties to be defunct, and certain political leaders were disqualified.[2]

Pakistan gained the status of Most Favored Nation from the United States following the Soviet invasion of Afghanistan in December 1979. On February 6, 1981, the Movement for Restoration of Democracy

2. "Martial Law Under General Zia-ul-Haq," *Pakistan Today*, June 1, 2003, https://storyofpakistan.com/martial-law-under-general-zia-ul-haq.

was established to return democracy to Pakistan. Finally, after the nomination of Muhammad Khan Junejo as Prime Minister of Pakistan on March 20, 1985, Junejo fulfilled his promise of lifting the martial law and restoring fundamental rights. Later on, Prime Minister Junejo's government attempted to restore democracy under the dictator's supervision.

While my parents were in jail, my older brother (who was only three years older than me) and I were at home alone, and from that point on, we raised ourselves. That was a crash course in learning how to lead our own lives and rely on ourselves.

Our lives changed drastically after that. Throughout those years, my brother and I spent a lot of time visiting our parents in jail. And instead of enjoying downtime at that age doing fun things with my friends, I had to spend vacation time and holidays working multiple jobs to earn a living. Life is the best teacher; you sometimes learn things you never expected.

Our relatives visited us sometimes, but no one moved in to live with us permanently. However, one of my uncles (Shakir Dad Khan, my father's elder brother) who was like a father figure to my brother and I, extended himself and tried to be with us as much as possible. His entire family provided unconditional support to us throughout our challenging years. They were always there for us. Every time my parents were released from jail and got to go home, they would go protest for restoration of democracy again and get arrested within a few days. They were fighting for a great cause, so my brother and I never let our parents feel that we could not manage on our own. Although we often felt miserable, and terrified at first, we assured our parents that we were doing fine. And we were. I started seeing the traces of leadership in me. I became the captain of my cricket team, and we did well as a team. Albeit I didn't exactly know what leadership was, I liked the sense of responsibility and winning.

This situation had a profound effect on me, and more so on my brother. From that point forward, I have always been keenly aware that your life, and the world around you, can change in an instant. We can never get too comfortable.

Some lessons are better experienced personally than read about in a book or blog post.

NEW YORK CITY: GREAT EDUCATION AND A CRASH COURSE IN SURVIVAL

Both my brother and I came to the United States to pursue higher education before our twentieth birthdays. Coming to this country was a much different experience for us. I clearly remember my mixed feelings the night before my flight to New York. On one hand, I was excited about the experience I was about to face, living in a new country. On the other hand, I was sad to leave my parents behind because their struggle for democracy was still in progress. I was most concerned about my mother because I was very close to her. She was the most determined person I have ever met.

The conversation I had with my mother the night before my departure was the most profound discussion I have ever had, even to this day. I could see her hiding tears and controlling emotions, all to give me the strength to start a new chapter in my life. Mothers are a gift of life; mine was the greatest gift.

That night, she did an amazing job of concealing her feelings about my departure. Asian mothers are laser-focused when it comes to education for their children. She realized that my moving far away from her was in my best interest; I might be safer in the United States. Of course, the main purpose was for me to get a higher education, but the United States provided opportunities that I would not have received if I had stayed behind.

I arrived in New York on January 18, 1985. My brother was already living here and studying. I was excited to join my brother and start a new life in New York, not realizing that the toughest days were ahead of me. Pursuing full-time education with limited finances and surviving in New York City was an interesting yet rewarding experience. In hindsight, the four years I spent going to college, working, and being unable to spend a single afternoon at home was a difficult yet exciting experience.

By the time I graduated, things had changed in my life, and also in Pakistan. Democracy was restored there, and my parents served as cabinet members in the government. At my graduation, both of my parents joined me, and this time. my mother couldn't hold her emotions. The tears in her eyes were tears of joy and gratification. I earned a business degree, but more importantly, a crash course in survival. Those skills later became a great seed of leadership that would stay with me forever.

New York City is a great place to learn about life. It teaches you how to survive, thrive, and lead—all while having fun. Most importantly, you can learn how to appreciate and embrace diversity. Interestingly, diversity became my business. I was fortunate to learn about so many cultures and how the land of opportunity opens to anyone and everyone. The reason people survive and thrive in New York City is because they learn how to adapt. Of course, I'm not saying that New York City is the only place in the world to live up to your potential. However, I will always have a biased opinion about New York City. I may need another book for that—maybe the next one.

I truly believe this is where leaders are made and destroyed. Pakistan and my parents' guidance planted the seed of leadership, but New York allowed it to grow. By no means am I claiming to be a seasoned leader; I am simply becoming a better student of leadership each and every day.

I consider our struggling teenage years as the most valuable years, in terms of a learning curve. My brother and I often talk about those years and value them now, even more. Life is the best teacher and always gives us options. We can complain about what we don't have, or we can celebrate what we do have. That tumultuous time taught us to be more resilient and focused. No moment in history is ever repeated. Good students use every moment as a learning opportunity and prepare themselves for when it is time to realize their dreams.

Our tough days are behind us, and both my brother and I survived the storm. I feel fortunate to have experienced that professional gratification.

My brother was far more focused in his career and life priorities than I was. When he graduated from Harvard Law school, he received many lucrative offers from several law firms. To everyone's surprise, he decided to move back to Pakistan. I clearly remember our discussion about staying in the United States to earn a good living; that opportunity offered far more growth opportunities than Pakistan.

His answer was simple and left me speechless. He said, "We are only two brothers. You have settled in the United States, and if I also do that, our parents will be alone in Pakistan. I don't want to do that."

He moved back to Pakistan and began his professional career, albeit a quite humble one in the beginning. He continued his professional growth and did fairly well. He became an extremely successful lawyer and also the 33rd and 35th Attorney General for Pakistan. More importantly, he spent more time with our parents. Our mother passed away at a young age in 2000.

Today, my biggest regret in life is not spending enough time with my mother. Some things in life are not replaceable.

THE CONSEQUENCES OF FAILING TO ADAPT

History is replete with examples of companies that enjoyed long-term success but then crumbled when they failed to adapt to changing times. Kodak is a prime example.

The Eastman Kodak Company was established in 1888 in Rochester, New York. It did very well throughout the twentieth century, becoming the leader in photographic film. But as people began to use digital cameras and smartphones to take photos, Kodak failed to seize the momentum of that radical change.

Kodak filed for bankruptcy protection in 2012 and sold its patents before reemerging as a much smaller company in 2013. Scott Anthony, the author of *Dual Transformation: How to Reposition Today's Business While Creating the Future*, says Kodak saw the changes coming but didn't change its business on a large enough scale to excel in the digital market. A Kodak engineer created the first prototype of a digital camera in 1975, but the company didn't invest resources in developing it fully.[3]

Anthony writes, "Companies often see the disruptive forces affecting their industry. They frequently divert sufficient resources to participate in emerging markets. Their failure is usually an inability to truly embrace the new business models the disruptive change opens up. Kodak created a digital camera, invested in the technology, and even understood that photos would be shared online. Where they failed was in realizing that online photo sharing *was* the new business, not just a way to expand the printing business."

Blockbuster is another example of a company that failed to adapt to changing technology. The company went out of business for failing to ride the wave of digital streaming of movies.

Companies and leaders who fail to adapt their offerings will be replaced by those who are more innovative.

---

3. "Kodak's Downfall Wasn't About Technology," Scott D. Anthony, *Harvard Business Review*, July 15, 2016, https://hbr.org/2016/07/kodaks-downfall-wasnt-about-technology.

Here are a few more examples of ways in which disruption of the norm is happening in all types of industries:

1. **Lodging**—For decades, the lodging industry operated as usual, under the arrogant belief that it could not be challenged. But then a company named Airbnb emerged on the scene, challenging the status quo, even though the company owned no significant real estate property.

   Before the emergence of Airbnb, if anyone went to Marriott or Hilton and told them that you may get a new competitor who owns no real estate, the leadership at both Marriott and Hilton would have laughed at the messenger.

2. **Transportation**—Higher-ups in the transportation industry thought any company that wanted to compete with its mega-leaders would need a lot of vehicles in its fleet. But then came Uber, which surged to success—without owning *any* vehicles.

3. **Retail**—Walmart had larger inventories of products than any other company. Alibaba and Amazon both changed the retail landscape to an online marketplace with no brick-and-mortar retail stores. Now Amazon is opening brick-and-mortar stores. They are adapting to consumers' changing preferences. The leaders of these companies don't just understand changing trends, environments, and consumers; they are responding to them.

We are living in a much different world today, and we can no longer take anything for granted. That includes leadership. You might have loads of experience as your asset, but ambitious young guns can walk in with little or no experience and assume control, fueled by their imagination, resilience, tenacity, and desire to be successful. We must evolve to remain competitive, and we must be prepared for the unexpected.

A POST-COVID ERA: THE NEW CHALLENGE FOR LEADERS

I started this book pre-COVID-19 and, as this book went to press, the world still had not fully recovered from COVID-19. Most of the people alive may have not witnessed the state of wretchedness, despondency, forlornness, and gloominess the world experienced during the pandemic. Yet new leaders emerged in the fields of healthcare, community services, and other areas.

A Case Study Failure of Global Leadership Handling COVID-19

COVID-19 was and is a unique phenomenon and possibly among the greatest test of leadership. Sadly, most leaders failed miserably at handling the pandemic. Indeed, the world was faced with an unprecedented challenge that practically impacted around the world.

The world is approaching loss of nearly 5 million human lives, and we are not even two years into the pandemic. The United States leads the death tolls followed by Brazil, India, Mexico, Peru, and Russia. In fact, these six countries together accounted for half of the known global death tally. Interestingly, China has been missing from the top casualty list as they have reported just over 4,600 deaths, and the COVID-19 initiated from Wuhan, China. Could China, India, and some other countries have done something differently to contain the spread of the virus and the variant globally? In my opinion, this was a collective failure in leadership.

The world is experiencing leadership bankruptcy

While I'm not throwing direct punches at all political leaders of these countries and I'm also not holding them fully responsible for the spread of COVID-19, we must identify leadership gaps in handling the pandemic effectively. I have identified five critical areas where the leaders failed or succeeded

1. Problem assessment
2. Identifying the best team
3. Developing proper strategy
4. Transparent communication
5. Executing the strategy and monitoring

We also must consider many other factors that came into play while handling the pandemic. The following factors played a critical role in fighting against the COVID-19 for many countries around the world.

1. Resources
2. Infrastructure
3. Overall population and Density
4. Location
5. Population mindset

Most of the countries who did well with COVID-19 were smaller countries and some with enough resources. I will never take away the credit from these leaders who managed the pandemic well irrespective of the size of these countries or the resources available to them. I did a closer case study on Pakistan and how they handled COVID-19 compared to other countries with large population.

Pakistan did extremely well with COVID-19 considering the challenges they faced. Pakistan is the 5th largest country in the world in terms of population. However, Pakistan is the 22nd largest economy in terms of purchasing power parity (PPP), and the 45th largest in terms of nominal gross domestic product (GDP). Pakistan's GDP per capita of $1,543 in 2020–21 ranks 154th in the world and giving it a PPP GDP per capita of $5,839 in 2021, which ranks 132nd in the world.

Source: https://en.wikipedia.org/wiki/Economy_of_Pakistan

Bottom line, Pakistan is a developing country with limited resources, poor infrastructure, and high population density with neighbors like Afghanistan, China, India, and Iran—all these neighbors served as epicenter of pandemic. A critical mass in Pakistan didn't see COVID-19 as a big threat and many people did their best to embrace the pandemic through their sheer negligence.

So, what was the reason for a lower death toll from the pandemic. Besides, a bit of luck, I would credit Pakistan's leadership, especially Prime Minister Imran Khan who took a firm stand on fighting COVID-19 smartly. I personally met Prime Minister, President, and a few other leaders in the government. The president of Pakistan, Dr. Arif Alvi, who is a dentist by profession, took a proactive approach and emphasized through public service messages to take precautions throughout the pandemic. I also met Mr. Asad Umar, federal minister for planning, development, reforms, and special initiatives. Mr. Umar is also leading Pakistan National Command and Operation Center (NCOC), the nerve center to synergize and articulate unified national efforts against COVID-19.

During my conversation with Mr. Umar, I asked him the reason for Pakistan's success in fighting the pandemic. Mr. Umar shared the five-point strategy that helped them so far.

1. Clarity—Pakistan's Prime Minister Imran Khan clearly saw the pandemic as a long-term challenge, and he made a firm decision to not go for a complete shut down as it may damage the weak economy. He opted for a smart lockdown keeping the economic activities on a limited basis while providing livelihood, especially to working-class population, many of whom worked on daily wages. This kept the economy going.

2. Defining metrics—Mr. Asad Umar defined failure simply as being unable to provide ventilators to those in need along with the ability to cope with the system. Many countries that registered high death tolls saw the near collapse of their medical infrastructure. So far, Pakistan's healthcare, which is feeble to begin with, has not collapsed yet.

3. Execution—NCOC had adopted a centralized approach in executing their strategy. We must keep in mind that Pakistan is a large country with many provinces and territories, and not all of them are ruled by the same political party that controls the federal government. The political agenda often drive them to disagree with each other. However, NCOC seemed to be aligned with all the provincial governments in executing their strategy.

4. Equity—They focused their decisions based on data, not on anecdotes or partisan politics. This was the key in gaining trust in a society where trust deficit prevails. Like most developing countries, people in Pakistan have limited trust in government programs. NCOC made efforts to ensure that all the resources are allocated based on need, not on political affiliation.

5. Transparent communication—Prime Minister Imran Khan took the lead in communicating directly and regularly with the people of Pakistan. It is critical to provide transparent information in a timely and simplified manner. People need to hear from their leaders and subject matter experts to gain the confidence in overcoming the challenges. NCOC has also provided communication to public on a regular basis and also developed website with live updates.

While the pandemic is far from over globally, I have personally witnessed how the government of Pakistan and many other nongovernmental organizations (NGOs) fought against COVID-19. However, the people of Pakistan did not take the pandemic as seriously as they should have. Many people in Pakistan didn't follow the guidelines strictly, and some didn't even believe in the pandemic. We find that cluster in every country.

Despite all these challenges, Pakistan produced much better fight than the countries with a lot more resources and effective medical infrastructure. This was a test of leadership and things may have easily gone haywire as it did in Pakistan's neigboring countries. Countries like New Zealand, Norway, Singapore, and others who have managed COVID-19 well deserve all the credit. However, these are small countries with sound infrastructure and educated population. On the other hand, Pakistan had all the red flags to fail in fighting the pandemic. So far, Pakistan has done well, and their leadership deserves all the credit.

I would also like to acknowledge the role of Ehsaas, a program launched by the government of Pakistan to reduce inequality, invest in people, and lift lagging districts around the country. Prime Minister Imran Khan is fully supportive of this program, and Dr. Sania Nishtar, special assistant on poverty alleviation and social safety to the Prime Minister of Pakistan, is leading this program. Ehsaas played a critical role during the pandemic by providing financial support to those who lost their livelihoods as a result of the COVID-19 pandemic. This served as a financial life line to many poor families.

I would remiss if I don't acknowledge the hard work of our healthcare fraternity around the world. They did an amazing job and far exceeded the expectation. The world would have completely collapsed if our healthcare professionals were not there. Also, the incredibly quick turnaround in developing and administering the vaccine is nothing short of a miracle. Our scientists and the entire pharma industry along with the government authorities approving the vaccine deserves a standing ovation. Last but not least, our global leaders who ensured that the vaccines are made available to all their eligible citizens in a timely and convenient manner are also the real heroes. Thanks for your leadership!

SUMMARY

- A leader should not panic and should develop an approach to overcome the challenge.
- A leader must be flexible enough to adapt with changing times but firm enough to get things done.
- Every challenge will leave an opportunity, smart leaders know how to leverage that opportunity.

QUOTES BY TARIQ KHAN

Losing to an ignorant person is always a win.

Age 0 to 25, we want to look older and 25 and over, we want to look younger.

CHAPTER 2

Eleven Leadership Myths

CHAPTER LEARNING OBJECTIVES

1. Analyze misconceptions about leadership.
2. Understand *classic leadership* and evaluate its relevance to today's business environment.
3. Recognize why today's businesses need adaptive leadership.

The world has changed rapidly in the past couple of decades, and more so after the life-altering pandemic, that it can be difficult to keep up. Technology and demographics have changed everything from the way we communicate to the way companies earn money. Many people say COVID-19 has taken us back many years, but I think it has taken us forward many years. The technology that facilitates virtual work life evolved quickly.

To understand how leaders can excel in the new landscape, we first need to debunk some myths about leadership. Here is my perspective on eleven common leadership myths.

MYTH #1: ENTREPRENEURSHIP IS THE SAME AS LEADERSHIP

One aspect of leadership that many people misunderstand is that entrepreneurship is not the same as leadership.

In past decades, people had to follow a protocol before becoming leaders in the corporate world. They had to "pay their dues" and move up the ranks of an organization. Plus, the throne of leadership was reserved mostly for older people with ample experience. It was like the military—you cannot be a general in your first five years in the armed services. The classically trained leaders of the past have been through a whole cycle of leadership, often spanning decades.

But today, anyone can be a leader at any age, without following any sort of protocol. Some of the wealthiest people in today's world graduated from college less than five years ago—or dropped out of college. And, although some wildly successful entrepreneurs have found themselves successful in ventures, some of them lack leadership.

For example, Mark Zuckerberg cofounded Facebook with a Harvard University classmate in 2004, when he was only twenty years old. By age thirty-four, he had amassed a fortune worth $66 billion. Zuckerberg took Facebook public on May 18, 2012. The initial public offering (IPO) raised $16 billion, making it the biggest tech IPO in history at the time. Zuckerberg became the 29th richest person on earth overnight.[1]

According to *Forbes*, Zuckerberg was the fifth-richest person on the planet as of January 13, 2021, with a net worth of approximately $92.2 billion.[2]

But recent scandals that have emerged regarding the company's business practices indicate, in my opinion, a lack of leadership.

Shortly after the 2016 U.S. presidential election, Facebook found that 126 million Americans probably saw Russia-funded posts intended to sway their votes. Then, in March 2018, #DeleteFacebook started trending after the founder of a data-analytics company called Cambridge Analytica came forward to say that it had harvested data from more than 50 million users' profiles—which Facebook later increased to 87 million—and used it to target voters during the 2016 election after being hired by the Trump campaign.[3]

The bottom line is that as an entrepreneur, you have proven that you can start a company and, in many cases, sustain a company. Does that make you a leader? No, it makes you an entrepreneur. Many successful leaders have never been entrepreneurs, although many entrepreneurs have become successful leaders.

Entrepreneurship is about innovating and starting an entity, whereas *leadership* is about improving and taking that entity to a new place.

MYTH #2: YESTERDAY'S "CLASSIC" LEADERSHIP LESSONS WILL ALWAYS BE RELEVANT

Another misunderstanding about leadership is that the most effective strategies will not necessarily continue to be effective in the future. The CEOs of past decades have impressive track records, but they might not necessarily excel in today's highly technical, global, fast-moving business environment.

1. "Mark Zuckerberg: A Look at the Life, Career, and Controversies Surrounding One of the Richest People in the World," Prachi Bardwaj, *Business Insider,* April 24, 2018, https://www.businessinsider.com/mark-zuckerberg-facebook-fabulous-life-career-photos-2017-4.
2. "Mark Zuckerberg's Portfolio," T. K. McDonald, Investopedia, updated January 14, 2021, https://www.investopedia.com/articles/personal-finance/042516/what-mark-zuckerbergs-portfolio-looks-fb-msft.asp.
3. "Mark Zuckerberg: A Look at the Life, Career, and Controversies Surrounding One of the Richest People in the World," Prachi Bardwaj, *Business Insider*, April 24, 2018, https://www.businessinsider.com/mark-zuckerberg-facebook-fabulous-life-career-photos-2017-4.

For example, Jack Welch was the chairman and CEO of General Electric between 1981 and 2001. Under his leadership, GE stock went up 4,000 percent, making it the most valuable corporation in the world at the time.[4] Warren Buffett runs Berkshire Hathaway, which owns more than sixty companies. He has promised to give away more than ninety-nine percent of his fortune. So far, Buffett has donated $35 billion, much of it to the foundation of his friends, Bill and Melinda Gates. Buffett's net worth was $85.1 billion as of December 2018, and he is now eighty-eight years old.[5]

But young people who graduate from college today typically may not consider people like Welch or Buffett as ideal leaders. They look up to the CEOs of today, such as Elon Musk, Mark Zuckerberg, and Jeff Bezos. These people are extremely successful, but we cannot say that all of them are great leaders because they have not stood the test of time yet. Facebook was founded in 2004. Tesla was incorporated in 2003, and Elon Musk became the CEO in 2008. Amazon.com has a little more history; Jeff Bezos founded the company in 1994.

None of these wildly successful companies have experienced long cycles of challenges and opportunities. They have not seen their first big challenge. As a result, the young people who are entering the workforce have an unrealistic expectation or view of leadership. To them, leadership looks a lot like overnight success without paying any "dues."

In 2004, Zuckerberg was talking to venture capitalists about raising money. A company called Sequoia Capital reached out to him. A *Business Insider* article says, "But Zuckerberg had no intention of considering an investment from Sequoia. That's because he had hired, and become friends with, Napster cofounder Sean Parker. Sequoia had invested in Parker's start-up Plaxo, and it hadn't gone well. There was bad blood." But Zuckerberg scheduled the meeting anyway, with a prank in mind. He showed up late to the meeting with Sequoia wearing pajamas and proceeded to show a PowerPoint presentation titled "The Top Ten Reasons You Should Not Invest."[6]

Needless to say, he did not receive funding from Sequoia. But he did phenomenally well without it.

As a result, many young people figure that if Mark Zuckerberg can go meet with a big investment company in his pajamas, they can do it, too. They think they can just come up with an innovative idea, google the names of some venture capitalists, and become a billionaire in no time at all.

In addition, a lot of people mistakenly think entrepreneurs are automatically leaders. There is a big difference. Creating a successful start-up does not equate to leading other people to greatness.

Leaders are responsible for many people and their livelihood, well-being, and survival. We often assume that the person who is in a leading role is a leader. But just because someone makes it to the top leadership slot doesn't mean he or she is a true leader. I call these people "necessary evils" who keep the real leaders happy and stroke their egos. They are good at pleasing people but not at leading people and companies to greatness. They do not create and execute a vision that leads to improvement in a situation. It takes innovation to extend one's vision beyond people, products, services, and placement.

---

4. "Jack Welch: 'I Fell in Love,'" *60 Minutes on CBS*, March 24, 2005, https://www.cbsnews.com/news/jack-welch-i-fell-in-love/.
5. "#3 Warren Buffett," *Forbes*, December 11, 2018, https://www.forbes.com/profile/warren-buffett/#3b06a3b74639.
6. "The Story of Sequoia Capital's $3 Billion 'Revenge' on Mark Zuckerberg," Nicholas Carson, *Business Insider*, February 20, 2014, https://www.businessinsider.com/how-much-sequoia-made-on-whatsapp-2014-2.

MYTH #3: SUCCESSFUL LEADERS ARE GOOD LEADERS

A third misunderstanding about leadership is that successful leaders are good leaders. In my opinion, leadership is an activity that motivates people to act outside their comfort zones and inspire other people to follow them into often uncharted territory. Leaders get things done through other people. Every boss, every entrepreneur, and every manager is not necessarily a leader.

Leadership is about commitment. It's about responsibility. Many personal coaches are great leaders. Most of the mothers in this world are great managers and great leaders.

Adolph Hitler, Osama bin Laden, Kim Jung-un, Fidel Castro, and many other world leaders were successful leaders because they maintained control over their people, but they were not good leaders. They did not make the world a better place. There are people who still think otherwise, but that's a matter of opinion.

MYTH #4: ONE SUCCESS GUARANTEES FUTURE SUCCESS

An old saying goes, "You're only as good as your last mistake." This is true among some of the most well-known leaders of our time. Many leaders who were successful and considered good at one time failed to deliver results as expected at some point.

In the corporate world, Martin Winterkorn, former CEO of Volkswagen; Marissa Mayer, former CEO of Yahoo; Ron Johnson, the former CEO of JC Penney; and Mike Jeffries, former CEO of Abercrombie & Fitch, are just some of the people who were proven leaders at one time, but in their last gigs, they were not able to deliver what was expected of them.

MYTH #5: LIFE HAS BECOME MORE COMPLICATED

In today's world, everything is moving faster and becoming more competitive. Many would say that our world has also become more complicated, but I believe life is simpler than ever.

For example, when I was a kid, if I needed to learn about a topic, I had to go to the library and spend hours reading an encyclopedia and searching for other books on that topic. Then I had to use my insight to translate that knowledge into intelligence and decipher which details were relevant to me. With the advent of technology and the internet, we can research a topic in minutes. We have eliminated many steps in the process and significantly reduced the amount of effort needed.

Also, in the older days, if you needed to market a product or service, you had to have a substantial budget for marketing materials like print advertising, TV commercials, and Yellow Pages ads (young folks may not know Yellow Pages, google it). But today, anyone with a mobile device can upload a video free of charge and become an overnight success. Of course, it is not that simple, but there are enough examples of successful marketing campaigns without major investment.

Life has been simplified for us to an extent that was beyond anyone's expectation. Today's world is drastically different than it was decades ago. But this is the only world that millennials (people born between 1981 and 1996) and Generation Z (those born from the mid-1990s to the early 2000s) have ever known.

I am a member of Gen X (people born between 1965 and 1980), and we have to adapt. Adapting to something new and unfamiliar is always more difficult than growing up with it. A baby who is born today will grow up completely comfortable with technology, whereas many people in the Silent Generation, also called the Greatest Generation (those born between 1928 and 1945), struggle to communicate with their grandkids because they don't often text or use apps. Some Baby Boomers (those born between 1946 and 1964) struggle to become adept at new technology, too. I have seen many fearless leaders being scared of technology when they go up on the stage to speak.

If you grew up in the classic corporate environment that was the norm decades ago, you will need to learn new skills and adopt a new mindset to keep up with the pace of change. We have no idea where new advancements such as artificial intelligence (AI) will take us. But we need to be ready to respond to those changes.

The leaders who keep open minds and commit to continuous learning typically do an impressive job of leading multigenerational teams. Those leaders who resist change and refuse to adopt new methods often find themselves locking horns with team members who grew up with technology—the "digital natives"—and want to modernize their companies' operations.

Another aspect of significant change in today's world is the widening diversity in this country and around the world. The real winner in the 2018 midterm elections and 2020 presidential elections in the United States was not a political party; it was diversity. More women, people from the LGBTQIA+ community, and those representing diverse communities won elections and are now assuming leadership roles at the local, state, and federal levels. That is changing the whole canvas.

I believe most of us will end up working for younger people, many of them females, in the near future. When I entered the workforce, managers were older than the sales team and other staff members, and they were males. Today, in most of my graduate courses at NYU, more than seventy percent of the students are women.

Who knows? A few years from now, we might be supervising robots, or vice versa.

MYTH #6: LEADERSHIP IS ABOUT MAKING A PROFIT

Success is no longer about profit. It's much bigger than that. Are we leaving enough water for the next generations? Are we protecting people? Are people living longer? Are we creating and developing products, so no one has to die because of an auto accident? Or because of diabetes, a virus, or any other disease? These are all treatable conditions. A physician can be a leader who finds that cancer is totally treatable, even if he or she isn't surrounded by a huge staff of people.

Much of this shift in the way we view success comes from the younger generations. Millennials tend to value being of service more than they value making money. In fact, I have learned a lot more from my kids and my younger colleagues than I have from my senior folks.

According to all seven of Deloitte's Millennial Surveys, including the most recent one conducted in 2018, millennials overwhelmingly feel that business success should be measured in terms of more than financial performance—a view that Gen Z shares (eighty-three and eighty percent, respectively). Millennials realize profits are both necessary and a priority, but they believe that corporations should set out to achieve a broad balance of objectives that include the following:

- Making a positive impact on society and the environment
- Creating innovative ideas, products, and services
- Job creation, career development, and improving people's lives
- An emphasis on inclusion and diversity in the workplace[7]

One of the wealthiest people in the world, Bill Gates, exemplifies these traits that young people value.

If you had asked me to describe the ideal leader ten years ago, I would have said it was someone who can create things that people want but don't need or take us to a place where we cannot go ourselves.

But today, I view the ideal leader as someone who challenges the status quo and changes the world. Examples include Malala Yousafzai and Greta Thunberg; both became global leaders as teenagers. Malala Yousafzai is a Pakistani activist for female education and the youngest Nobel Prize laureate; she was born in 1997. Greta Thunberg is a Swedish environmental activist who is internationally known for challenging world leaders to take immediate action against climate change. She was born in 2003.

The classic model of leadership measured CEOs and companies on how much they improved the bottom line. It was all about the money. Times are changing, and the definition of leadership is being redefined. The gauge of success is shifting to measure the extent to which individuals and companies are leaving the world better than they found it.

I consider Microsoft founder Bill Gates to be a true leader—not because of his wealth and success in business, but because of what he's doing with his money. When he left Microsoft, he fully dedicated himself to the Bill and Melinda Gates Foundation.

One of the many projects Gates is involved is in the fight against malaria. I consider this remarkable because malaria doesn't even exist in the United States, where Gates lives. When he and his wife, at that time, Melinda, established the Bill and Melinda Gates Foundation in 2000, Gates began focusing on the eradication of malaria.

---

7. "The Deloitte Millennial Survey 2018," Deloitte, https://www2.deloitte.com/global/en/pages/about-deloitte/articles/millennialsurvey.html#.

He works with organizations around the world, particularly in Africa, where malaria was most prevalent, to develop innovative strategies to help prevent and cure malaria, including new insecticides, better bed nets, rapid diagnostic tests, improved drugs, drones to track mosquitoes, and even tools to genetically modify mosquitoes. In March 2018, Gates announced that the Bill and Melinda Gates Foundation would invest another $1 billion in the fight against malaria.[8]

Bill Gates says he has learned from Berkshire Hathaway, chairman and CEO Warren Buffet, that the true measure of success has nothing to do with money. Instead, they measure success by the strength of their personal relationships, as opposed to professional or financial milestones—whether or not the people they care about love them back.[9]

This shows Gates's ability to adapt because for years, he was entrenched in corporate environments in which success is based on benchmarking, metrics, and profit-and-loss statements. Once he entered the world of philanthropy, the measure of success was entirely different. Gates proved his leadership abilities in the corporate world by creating and leading Microsoft. Now he is focused on much bigger causes that can truly change the world.

Companies like Airbnb, Uber, Lyft, Blue Apron, Pinterest, WeWork, and Zillow aren't profitable, yet they are valued in billions of dollars. For many of these companies, the focus is on growth, not profit. Facebook didn't show any meaningful profit in the first seven years of its operation, and now it reports profit in billions of dollars.

The trends will continue to change, and good leaders will continue to adapt to create value.

MYTH #7: WORKERS ARE JUST AS LOYAL TODAY AS IN THE PAST

In the older days, people tended to stay with their employers for many years, often a lifetime. But today, job hopping is the norm. The 2018 Deloitte Millennials Survey reports that forty-three percent of millennials envision leaving their jobs within two years; only twenty-eight percent seek to stay beyond five years. Employed Gen Z respondents express even less loyalty, with sixty-one percent saying they would leave within two years if given the choice.[10]

Many older leaders are losing a lot of good talent because they are applying old expectations on this audience. The Deloitte report describes the approach leaders need to take to attract and retain young workers today: "Attracting and retaining millennials and Gen Z begins with financial rewards and workplace culture; it is enhanced when businesses and their senior management teams are diverse, and when the workplace offers higher degrees of flexibility. Those who are less than satisfied with their pay and work flexibility are increasingly attracted to the gig economy, especially in emerging markets."

8. "Bill Gates Pledges $1 Billion to Fight Malaria as Experts Fear Resurgence," Katherine Hignett, *Newsweek*, April 20, 2018, https://www.newsweek.com/bill-gates-malaria-finding-895363.
9. "There Is One Ultimate Measure of a Successful Life, According to Bill Gates and Warren Buffett, and It Has Nothing to Do with Money," Mark Abadi, *Business Insider,* January 5, 2019, https://www.businessinsider.com/bill-gates-warren-buffett-success-relationships-2019-1.
10. "The Deloitte Millennial Survey 2018," Deloitte, https://www2.deloitte.com/global/en/pages/about-deloitte/articles/millennialsurvey.html#.

We must redefine job loyalty. In the past, people stayed longer with companies, and they didn't have many reasons to leave and change their employer or profession. Yes, the incoming workforce don't see staying with the same company for years as a feather in their cap. Also, the companies have become heartless in letting people go. The feelings are mutual. Good leaders create an environment where people want to stay, and the organization wants to retain good talent.

Also, longevity in any position of leadership is no longer guaranteed the way it once was. In the older days, when people became doctors and finished their residencies, they were pretty much guaranteed lifetime employment. Leadership was the same way. Once you became a CEO, you could stay until you wanted to leave.

But today, corporate leadership is becoming more like politics, with "term limits." Every three or four years, you could be voted out. You could build a great company, but then two college roommates without many resources could challenge your business. This is why it is critical to adapt your leadership style and skills to thrive in today's changing times.

MYTH #8: TECHNOLOGY HAS MADE COMMUNICATION EASIER

Traditionally, our best leadership efforts came when we had face-to-face meetings with our team members. We were able to look in their eyes and gain their trust. Now, half or more of our team members might be working remotely, and at best, we might see them on a computer screen. There's no human touch, no handshake, no pat on the back. The COVID-19 pandemic forced most of the world to work virtually for many months.

I have never met some of the people that I have worked with in person, although, they live in same country as I do. We were quite comfortable working with people pre-COVID-19, the pandemic has just validated remote working. We have to accommodate our employees if we want to benefit from their talent.

When I decided to leave my first job, I went to see my senior leader. He looked into my eyes, held my hand, and said, "You are a valuable team player, now go back to work." I was unable to leave the job.

I can't do that with people I can't see. I'm not trained to have conversations like that on the phone or on a live chat. If I need something from them, they often say, "Let's Zoom." We run most meetings on Zoom now. All of us are getting very comfortable on digital screens. We have stopped calling people on the phone. And what happened to conference calls? "Let's Zoom" is the new "Let's Google."

Resisting the new way things are done will not make them go away. The people who are shaping the workforce today are the ones who will drive the way we communicate and do business. Regardless of what we learned in the past; we must adapt to the new order of things.

MYTH #9: SOCIAL MEDIA HAS ENHANCED OUR WELL-BEING

Social media is one of the most powerful resources of our time. Many leaders have tapped into the power of social media to hire talent and acquire clients.

But I believe we are seriously suffering because of social media. I consider our obsession with social media an epidemic.

If you look at the screen on your phone or device every few minutes, even without any alerts; if your mobile device accompanies you to the bathroom, even in the middle of the night, and if you look at the screen more than you don't, then you're seriously suffering from it. I know people who are extremely busy, but from 11:00 p.m. to 1:00 a.m., they're very active on social media, chatting and sharing videos and blogs with their friends. This is great entertainment. I don't want to downplay that, but it is robbing several hours a day from each one of us. That's the negative part.

Here's the positive part. The reason our smartphones and devices have become so popular is because they have replaced a lot of tools we were using.

In 2014, a writer and historian named Steve Cichon found a Radio Shack advertisement in a February 16, 1991, edition of the *Buffalo News* newspaper. Of the fifteen electronic items advertised, thirteen are now available on a smartphone, including a calculator, a radio, voice mail, a camera, a camcorder, and a tape recorder.[11]

Again, I'm not against social media. I consider it one of the biggest innovations of our time. I'm against *obsession* with the social media, which is quite close to a sickness. Remember, we were young, and our parents feared that TV will ruin our lives, it didn't, neither will social media. We will adapt and get over our obsession.

MYTH #10: THE INCREASE IN NEWS SOURCES MAKES US MORE INFORMED

One activity many of us enjoy on our phones and devices is reading news reports. In the past, there were a few major sources of news, and we accessed them from newspapers, magazines, the radio, or television. We could trust that news reported by Dan Rather or Peter Jennings on the nightly news was probably accurate.

But today, people get their news from Twitter, Facebook, Instagram, and other social media outlets. As soon as something happens, people post it. As a result, the general public has become the source of news. A lot of people are applauding this new ubiquitous access to news. But I think it is a problem because Facebook or Twitter cannot stand behind the news that's posted on their walls.

---

11. "Everything From This 1991 Radio Shack Ad You Can Now Do With Your Phone," Steve Cichon, *Huffington Post,* December 6, 2017, https://www.huffingtonpost.com/steve-cichon/radio-shack-ad_b_4612973.html.

As long as you're posting your personal photos on social media, that's fine. But if you generate information that could be detrimental in some way, then at some point in time, the state has to step in. Regulators will say, "You have a database of more than two billion people in this world. Now you know more about those people than they know about themselves." Companies that maintain vast databases of consumer data have an obligation to protect those data. We could argue that having an unregulated news environment makes us more informed. But we no longer can rely on the accuracy of news reports, and now it's more difficult to hold people accountable for "fake news."

Facebook can influence or even elect the next U.S. president, and I find that unacceptable—at least for now.

MYTH #11: EVERYTHING WE DO IS PRIVATE

When we sign up for many social media sites and check the box that says "I agree" without reading the legal disclaimer, we are, in essence, giving those sites permission to use our data any way they like. We can no longer expect privacy.

In April 2018, forty-four senators grilled Facebook CEO Mark Zuckerberg during five hours of testimony before the U.S. Senate about the Cambridge Analytica scandal. In early 2018, it was revealed that Cambridge Analytica had captured the personal data of millions of people's Facebook profiles without their consent and used it for political purposes.[12]

To make a point about user privacy concerns, Senator Dick Durbin from Illinois asked Zuckerberg if he would be comfortable sharing the name of the hotel he stayed in the previous night. Zuckerberg smiled and said no. The audience and panel of senators erupted in laughter at Zuckerberg's hesitancy to answer the question. Senator Durbin followed up with, "If you messaged anybody this week, would you share with us the names of the people you've messaged?"

Zuckerberg replied no, and Senator Durbin said, "I think that might be what this is all about: your right to privacy, the limits of your right to privacy, and how much you'd give away in modern America."

It doesn't make sense to me that Mark Zuckerberg is worried about people intruding into his privacy when he appears to be allowing Facebook users' privacy to be compromised or largely sharable.

But social media isn't the only medium that is tracking our personal data. Companies are tracking our movements every day. For example, if I park my car in a garage in New York City and get out of my car to walk to my office, an alert pops up on my phone that says, "It's a seven-minute walk to your office." Someone has tracked my behavior and knows the route I walk to my office every day. As long as I have my phone with me and it's on, these companies are tracking. They know which restaurants I like to eat at, and which places I like to shop. I think they have an unfair advantage.

12. "Awkwardness Ensues as Top Democratic Senator Asks Mark Zuckerberg if He'll Reveal What Hotel He Stayed at Last Night," Joe Perticone, *Business Insider,* April 10, 2018, https://www.businessinsider.com/dick-durbin-asks-mark-zuckerberg-what-hotel-he-stayed-at-2018-4.

In December 2018, *The New York Times* found that at least seventy-five companies receive anonymous, precise location data from apps whose users enable location services to get local news and weather or other information. Several of those businesses claim to track up to 200 million mobile devices in the United States, about half those in use in 2017. The database that Times reporters reviewed—a sample of information gathered in 2017 and held by one company—reveals people's travels in startling detail, accurate to within a few yards and in some cases updated more than 14,000 times a day. These companies sell, use, or analyze the data to cater to advertisers, retail outlets, and even hedge funds seeking insights into consumer behavior. It's a hot market, with sales of location-targeted advertising reaching an estimated $21 billion in 2018.[13]

So how does that relate to leadership? It has changed the environment in which we do business. Now CEOs aren't just selling products/services and trying to earn revenue. Today they are also fighting to protect their clients' and employees' personal data. They have to balance the power of innovation with the loss of people's privacy and protection.

How this will play in the new post-COVID-19 world, which is more virtual and data-dependent, remains to be seen.

Today's business environment is driven, in large part, by social media. Your social media followers know you almost as well as you know yourself (leaders included). You might have noticed that every now and then people you're connected with on social media recall situations and events you can't recall yourself. Your social media followers know your activities, your behavior, and your attitude—and your accounts keep accurate records on all of that!

SUMMARY

- The role of a leader is constantly changing. Leaders need to adapt to meet new challenges and opportunities.
- Your followers—and customers—are more demanding and expect more from their leaders than in the past.
- The role of social media cannot be underestimated.
- Resisting the new way things are done will not make them go away. The people who are shaping the workforce today are the ones who will drive the way we communicate and do business.

13. "Your Apps Know Where You Were Last Night, and They're Not Keeping It Secret," Jennifer Valentino-DeVries, Natasha Singer, Michael H. Keller, and Aaron Krolik, *The New York Times*, December 10, 2018, www.nytimes.com/interactive/2018/12/10/business/location-data-privacy-apps.html.

QUOTES BY TARIQ KHAN

A father learns many things from his daughter and teaches many things to his son.

The most expensive liability is ignorance, and the worst habit is arrogance.

CHAPTER 3

Leaders—Born or Made?

CHAPTER LEARNING OBJECTIVES

1. Learn the extent to which someone can learn to become an effective leader, as opposed to being born with leadership skills.
2. Understand the importance of recognizing and leveraging potential opportunities.
3. Gain insight into three leaders' views of the important characteristics of leaders who are able to adapt well to change.

Are leaders born or made? This question has been asked many times, and the opinions vary a lot. Most people agree it is a bit of both: we are born with some leadership traits, and we learn others. My opinion is different. I believe that almost every person is a born leader. In fact, we are all born with ideal leadership traits.

BABIES HAVE IDEAL LEADERSHIP TRAITS

You probably have never thought about babies having leadership qualities, but they do. Children under the age of two or three years have many of the traits that are common among the most effective leaders. Here are nine:

1. Babies are resilient. If they fall down, they get back up again.
2. They have a lot of confidence.
3. They can walk into anything and not be afraid. Fear is a learned behavior, so they will try anything because they don't know about danger.

4. They know how to delegate, assert their wishes, and communicate effectively, even if they cannot speak yet. If they need something, they will hand things to others or cry, and people will respond to their needs.

5. They are not afraid to say "No!" if they don't agree with something.

6. They trust the people around them.

7. They are extremely focused.

8. They are huge risk-takers.

9. They have a vision of what they want to accomplish.

As children get older, they learn qualities like caring and integrity from the people around them. Those are important leadership qualities as well. But soon, they lose touch with all those great leadership traits. Why is that? It's because parents rein their children in and tell them what to do and what not to do. "Don't touch that! Don't go in there! Don't talk right now!" Because parents want to keep their children safe, they are not great risk-takers, so they treat children very differently than they do adults.

We are a gifted species in many ways, but we are not self-sufficient. We are the only animals that need constant care for many years after birth. It takes human babies close to a year, or more, to learn how to walk, but most other animals walk within a couple of hours after birth. When a fish is born, the mother fish doesn't feed the baby; it goes out on its own. When a turtle is born on the beach, it finds its own way to the water. Humans can't even turn their heads or flip over for a few months after birth. By nature, we are dependent.

Our parents like to hold our hands as long as they can. We make our children dependent on us longer than we need to because we care about them and worry about what will happen to them if we let them try new experiences on their own. By doing that, we are stifling their creativity and squelching their leadership potential. We are discouraging creativity, innovation, and risk-taking.

Only a small percentage of children emerge from the limitations of childhood with their leadership potential still intact. Interestingly, children growing up under difficult circumstance, or without both parents, often learn to be resilient and do well in life. There are many successful people like Steve Jobs, Bill Clinton, LeBron James, Shaquille O'Neal, Lance Armstrong, Eric Clapton, Faith Hill, Demi Moore, Jack Nicholson, Pierce Brosnan, and Samuel L. Jackson to name a few who had challenging childhoods. These individuals were tenacious leaders who defied all odds and did well in life, despite a rough beginning. Those who are resilient and defy the norms tend to become leaders.

And they don't have to be adults to be influential leaders.

MALALA YOUSAFZAI: A STRONG LEADER AT JUST FIFTEEN YEARS OLD

On October 9, 2012, fifteen-year-old girl named Malala Yousafzai was on a bus in Swat Valley, Pakistan, riding from school back home. The Taliban stopped the bus. They recognized the girl and shot her and two other girls. The reason she was targeted and shot was because of her activism and her fight for young girls to have access to education.

She was shot in the head in an assassination attempt, but miraculously survived. Most people, after getting shot in the head, would try to stay out of trouble. But Malala continued her struggle. In fact, she made the right to education for girls her mission.

In 2014, at age seventeen, Malala became the youngest ever Nobel Prize laureate when she was the co-recipient of the 2014 Noble Peace Prize, along with Kailash Satyarthi of India. She was obviously born with leadership traits like resilience and a clear vision. With support from her family and with guidance from others, today Malala is a global leader who has a strong voice and following.

What happens in life is not always in our control, but how we react to a situation *is* in our control. Like many people, Malala could have easily adapted to the pressure to stay quiet and live a safer life. However, she wouldn't have become a global icon.

LEADERS MUST DEFINE THE BUSINESS CENTRIC

Great leaders are crystal clear about their objectives, goals, vision, mission, purpose, and the environment that want to create. You must know where you are going; otherwise, you can end up anywhere. The leaders should not only be clear about their business centric, but they should be able to communicate this and motivate their teams to help them to achieve this goal.

Good leaders are always clear about their priorities and the business culture they want to create. There are three major drivers that becomes the core of company businesses, and every leader should pick the centric of their business from the following:

1. Employee centric
2. Customer centric
3. Stockholders centric

It is important to define what kind of a culture you want to build in your organization. Leaders who are focused on an employee-driven company always put their employees as their top priority. They believe that happy employees make happy customers. One of my clients whom I have been coaching for a few years is a perfect example of building an "Employee First" culture. Shahed Islam and his wife Shahera Choudhury are founders of SJ Innovation, a software development company based in New York with global offices in Bangladesh, India, and Ukraine. I have known them for many years and coached them for a few years. I have seen an unconditional commitment and servant leadership for their employees in both Shahed and Shahera. For every decision they consider, they first think how this would impact their employees. SJ Innovation's motto is "Employee Happiness Generates Client Success" It is not only a website placeholder. They walk the talk every day by caring for their employees.

Amazon founder Jeff Bezos has built a company that is flawlessly customer centric. Bezos is known to have an empty seat at his company's important meetings to remind the decision-makers that the most important person in the meeting is the customer. Ask any customer of Amazon and they will endorse that Amazon is a truly customer-centric business.

Many publicly traded companies claim to be employee and customer centric, but they indeed are stockholder and board driven. Most of these companies look after the interests of their key stockholders and boards and publicly acknowledge their priority. While some companies may claim to have all three (employees, customers, and stockholders) as their top priorities, it is very difficult to do that. It is a leader's job to define the priority and develop a culture to drive that across the company.

LEADERS LEARN HOW TO DELEGATE

Now that we know that we were born with some leadership traits, let's learn about some traits we are not born with—delegation, for example.

Not everyone is born as a gifted delegator. Many leaders were managers or order takers before they became leaders. The skill of delegation does not always come from power given to you. With a planned approach, delegation can be self-acquired.

Imagine that you are sitting in a plane waiting to take off. A few hours later, you are still sitting in the plane on the runway, without any communication—no explanation for the flight delay.

Now imagine that one passenger stands up and refuses to accept the airline's treatment of passengers and successfully gets all passengers to leave the plane in protest. No one nominated this person to lead. He or she decided to accept the challenge, took the lead, and delegated others to follow him/her. He also assigned different tasks like asking one passenger to go in the back and communicate the walkout and ask another passenger to ensure that no one stays in the plane and other responsibilities to other people. Obviously, that person is gifted with leadership traits and knows how to use them.

Most of us have some leadership traits. But sadly, we don't realize we have those traits, so we miss opportunities to use them.

Not everyone is going to be a leader, and not everyone should become a leader. We can have leadership moments through our lives, though, and we can demonstrate leadership as needed. Leadership is liability and a commitment. It is an unpaid debt that reminds us to deliver on our responsibilities every day. People who are comfortable in their own space and not looking for any additional responsibilities should not become leaders.

GOOD LEADERS ADOPT GOOD HABITS: INSIGHTS FROM LEADERS I KNOW

Leadership is not a destination; it is a journey. You don't become leader and stop learning. If you do, it will be a sojourn. Leaders, by nature, are always in pursuit of improvement. A good leader always observes others and tries to pick good habits that can make him or her a better leader.

I have had an opportunity to work with some amazing managers and leaders. Almost every aspect of my leadership style has come from reading or learning from others.

Recently, I reached out to a few of my colleagues, and I found them to be quite disciplined in their approaches to work. Here are some highlights of their comments to me.

1. MARK HUG, FORMER CHIEF MARKETING OFFICER, PRUDENTIAL LIFE

I have known Mark for nearly ten years. He is a unique leader; he is an actuary by education and a marketer by profession. Mark always stood out to me as a thought leader who is clear in his approach. He has mastered the art of doing more with less time. I saw Mark doing that in his corporate job at Prudential. When he retired, I asked him to join my company as a senior advisor. I had an opportunity to work closely with him and personally witnessed how effectively he used his time. I asked Mark to share his thoughts on time management. Here is what he shared with me:

> The most valuable commodity in every leader's life is time. As responsibilities grow both at home and at work, the leader often has a growing anxiety of not having enough time to accomplish goals set forth. I recognized this early in my career and set some guideposts about how to manage it. These guideposts quickly allowed me to accomplish more in my life with much less time by forcing me to work smarter. The guideposts are as follows:
>
> 1. Family is always first. Nothing at the job is more important than family.
> 2. Have dinner with the family every night.
> 3. Never bring work home from the office.
> 4. Never work on weekends.
>
> Sound impossible? Well, it's not. Even in these times of working from home and doing business 100 percent online, this is possible. For forty years of my career, I was able to be home early and rarely work at night or on weekends. This guidepost allowed me to focus on my job fully while I was working and to focus on my family fully when I was not working. I managed my time accordingly.

Here are some of the hurdles that every leader face and what I did to get over those hurdles:

1. **Peer pressure:** I realized this is the single biggest driver for leaders to stay late at the office and work weekends. I can't tell you how awkward I felt leaving the office before every one of my peers. Nonetheless, with courage, you can do this and succeed in your career.

2. **Meetings:** These swallow up time so quickly. Rarely do meetings need to last more than fifteen or thirty minutes. If you want to brainstorm or just discuss topics randomly, then schedule time to do so, but avoid the meeting "black holes." I also made it a habit of coming into the office very early (6:30 a.m. or earlier) when no one was in the office, and I had no meetings. I could complete a lot of "heavy lifting."

3. **Emails/texts:** I would get hundreds of work-related emails and texts every day. Yet I found that I needed to read only about five percent of them. The other ninety-five percent were useless in progressing my projects. By skimming the communications instead of reading them fully, I could see at a glance which ones I could ignore. I also delegated tasks to others when I could. Delegation is often key, and it requires that you trust your team members to get the job done.

4. **Reports:** I used to receive reports that were dozens of pages long. I soon trained my staff and everyone around me that I would read only one-page reports. If a report couldn't sum up the issues and conclusions in one page, then the team didn't have a good-enough handle on the issue.

I followed these guideposts and "hurdle busters" religiously. I found myself having plenty of time to enjoy work and my family—to live a fulfilling life. Even today, I relish this work–life balance as I balance a robust consulting business, the relaxation of retirement, and serving my community.

2. VINCE VITIELLO, PRESIDENT, NEW AMERICA MARKETING; FORMER LEADERSHIP ROLES AT METLIFE, ALLIANZ, AND NATIONAL LIFE

I have known Vince for nearly thirty years and have worked closely with him in many capacities. I had an opportunity to work with Vince at MetLife, and he also joined my company, GDM, as president for a few years. Vince has always brought energy and a positive attitude to work every day. He was a successful sales leader and motivated many people, including me. I asked Vince to share his secret for his professional energy. Here is what he shared:

> I don't think energy is derived on a daily basis by gulping down a few caffeine shots. (Although that may help.). It's been my belief it starts with a dream—big or small, but something that gets you excited to get up in the morning. Next, think of what the finish line looks like. Those two steps are a great start, but now come the more difficult tasks.
>
> I like to break my goals into quarters. Then I write down my weekly goals—always on a Sunday morning. In the past twenty-five years, I don't think I've missed my self-imposed weekly goal-setting time.

> Last, the easy part. Before bed each evening, I simply write the three personal and business goals I plan to accomplish the next day. My personal goal could be as simple as getting a haircut, my business goals typically are geared to move my business and team forward. This daily goal setting has woken me up in the morning, tasks in hand, and so anxious to scratch of each one as the morning progresses. I remain focused, with a sense of confidence that creates energy for bigger and grander goals!
>
> Then another cup of coffee!

3. AAMIR CHALISA, MANAGING DIRECTOR, FUTURITY FIRST INSURANCE GROUP

I have known Aamir for nearly thirty years, both in personal and professional capacities. He is one of my best friends and an amazing individual. The most striking thing about Aamir is that he gets the job done. I always say, "Don't give anything to Aamir if you don't want it done." I have worked with Aamir at MetLife and Nationwide, and we have traveled the world together. I always appreciate his sense of responsibility. I asked him to share his method to the madness on getting things done. Here is what he shared:

> Good leaders take responsibility and never place blame. Everyone is ready to take credit when things go well. Yet, it is all finger pointing at others when things go south. Blame is easy. Bad leaders blame someone or something else. But blame is unproductive and detrimental. Being a productive leader means taking responsibility. Truly stepping up and taking responsibility creates the opportunity to innovate and build value. So don't place blame. Take responsibility!
>
> Blame is unproductive … it is a post-mortem, backward-looking exercise. Responsibility is forward-looking.

Now, all these leadership traits, including work–life balance from Mark, energy from Vince, and a must-do attitude from Aamir, are a combination of both innate and learned characteristics. I have known all these individuals for long enough to say that they were born with these traits, but they really came to excel at them by practicing them regularly and religiously.

LEADERSHIP IS ABOUT LEVERAGING OPPORTUNITY

Many of us are born with some leadership traits, but we don't fully leverage them. A person born in a remote village may have incredible vision and intuition, but if they never applied it to make a difference to others, then it is an opportunity not availed. And that is OK. Not everyone wants to be a leader, is a leader, or should be a leader.

Good leaders always excel at their innate leadership traits and work hard on learning others. Other leaders were not gifted with innate leadership traits; they acquired them through their commitment to learning them.

In my opinion, LeBron James, of the LA Lakers, is among the greatest basketball players in the history of the NBA. He is naturally gifted, and players like him are born once in many decades. Of course, his tenacity and work ethic got him where he is, but his talent was more natural.

On the other hand, Jimmy Butler, of the Miami Heat, is another great basketball player who worked extremely hard to get where he is. I do not believe Jimmy was as naturally talented as many other players, but his endurance and perseverance earned him his status as a great player.

Whether your traits are innate or learned, you will excel at them by practicing, refining, and leveraging them to produce the best outcomes.

SUMMARY

- Leaders can have both innate and learned leadership skills; the key is to practice and refine them.
- Delegation is an important leadership skill, and most leaders have to learn it.
- Leaders, by nature, are always in pursuit of improvement.
- Effective leaders exercise discipline to manage work–life balance, derive energy from having a dream, and take responsibility for whatever happens.

QUOTES BY TARIQ KHAN

There are two ways to solve a problem: simple and complicated. Interestingly, complicated is more popular.

Most leaders fail changing the culture of an organization, unless their family owns the business.

CHAPTER 4

Do You Have Critical Leadership Traits?

CHAPTER LEARNING OBJECTIVES

1. Examine twelve traits of leadership and an additional three traits that leaders need in changing times.
2. Complete a Leadership Traits Self-Assessment to score your self-perceived strength in these thirteen traits.
3. Learn why leadership traits by themselves are not a complete foundation for a future in leadership.

Leadership is simply the art of seeing things other people cannot see, creating a team composed of talented people, and then getting out of their way to let them achieve the vision. As leaders, our job is to coach others, provide resources, and open doors. Leaders create opportunities for others, find the most talented person for each role, and inspire others to achieve greatness.

But the leadership traits that served us well yesterday are not enough for us to thrive in the future. Tomorrow's leaders will need to be innovatively visionary so they can create products and services that do not exist today and distribute them to places where we have no access to today. They will need to adapt quickly as technology evolves.

In the past, leaders found solutions to the problems that came our way. Today's leaders respond to new problems and then find the solutions for them while improving the lives of others.

Next, let's look at twelve traits of leadership and an additional three traits that leaders need in changing times. At the end of this chapter is a Leadership Traits Self-Assessment you can use to score your self-perceived strength in these thirteen traits. Then you can take steps to strengthen those traits you feel need improvement.

TWELVE TRAITS OF LEADERSHIP

How do you know whether or not you are a leader? Are you the only person besides your mother who thinks you're a leader?

As discussed in the previous chapter, many of us are born leaders. Babies have ideal leadership traits, but we tend to lose them as we grow up because we typically don't nurture them.

There is no leadership thermometer that can tell you if you're a leader or not. However, there are a few traits and traces of leadership that I believe are common among the most effective leaders. In my opinion, the following twelve traits describe the leaders of today:

1. Innovative vision
2. A risk-taking mentality
3. Resilience
4. Caring for others
5. Transparency in communication
6. Confidence
7. Intuition
8. The ability to inspire others
9. Patience
10. Self-control
11. Integrity
12. The ability to delegate

Let's look at each trait in detail.

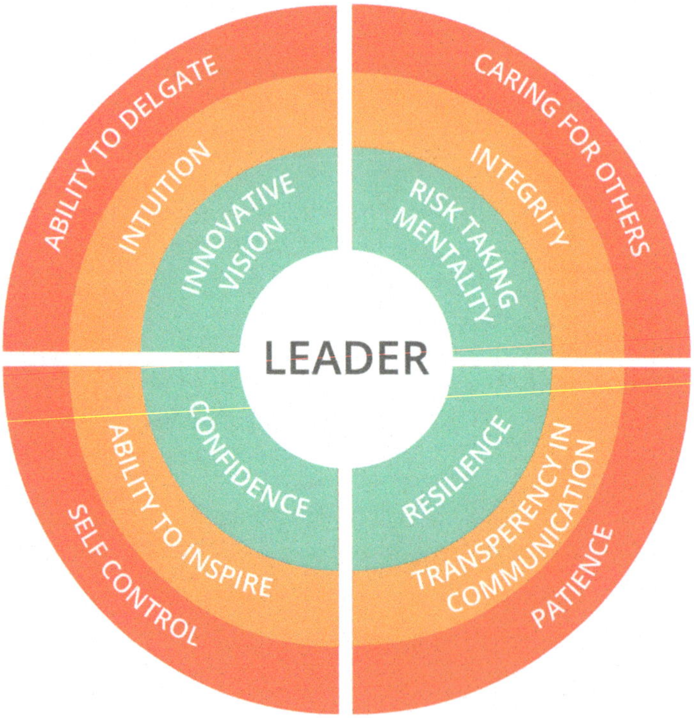

1. INNOVATIVE VISION

Being a visionary has always been an essential ingredient of leadership. Many leaders aren't even prepared to think about innovative vision. And when they do, others fail to share their vision. Sometimes, people around us will even ridicule us for our innovative vision, claiming it is unrealistic. That's because they are not looking far enough into the future to see the possibilities.

Mark Zuckerberg founded Facebook in 2005, with this mission: "To give people the power to share and make the world more open and connected." In 2017, Facebook revised the mission statement like this: "To give people the power to build community and bring the world closer together."[1]

Imagine—as a young college student, Zuckerberg envisioned connecting the world. And today, the platform has connected 2.7 billion people around the world happily, and virtually for free. Similarly, Google founders Larry Page and Sergey Brin envisioned providing access to world's information. Let's not forget Elon Musk's vision of taking people to Mars and making gas cars like steam engines. All these ideas sounded unrealistic and impossible to some people, but these dynamic leaders with innovative vision could see the future.

Leaders have always been visionary. The new requirement today is to be innovative beyond imagination.

2. A RISK-TAKING MENTALITY

I think *avoiding* risk is the biggest risk. I have seen many leaders who were conservative in their approach, but they are not known for their legacies. True leaders are remembered by people and by history. I'm not saying that conservative leaders are not good leaders, but it is difficult for someone to be a leader without taking risks.

Everyone's level of risk tolerance varies. In the older times, big risk-taking was not a norm of leadership. Risk-taking could be viewed as reckless, whereas "towing the line" was considered wise. In changing times, though, risk-taking is the main ingredient of leadership.

Every story you hear about successful leaders, whether they are leaders in politics, business, or civics, reveals an element of risk-taking.

In October 2018, *Forbes* magazine named Amazon founder and CEO Jeff Bezos as the richest person in the world, with a net worth of more than $160 billion. Until then, Bill Gates had held the top spot on that list for twenty-four years. Bezos is also the first person to appear in the ranks with a fortune of more than $100 billion.[2]

---

1. Facebook Inc.'s Mission Statement & Vision Statement (An Analysis), Nathaniel Smithson, February 25, 2019, http://panmore.com/facebook-inc-vision-statement-mission-statement.
2. "The Definitive Ranking of the Wealthiest Americans," Luisa Kroll and Kerry A. Dolan, *Forbes*, October 3, 2018, https://www.forbes.com/forbes-400/#52edc1a27e2f.

In 1994, Bezos was a senior vice president at D. E. Shaw & Co., a Wall Street–based investment banking firm. Eight years out of college at Princeton, Bezos was thirty years old, and while his career in finance was lucrative, he was personally unfulfilled. Then he read a report forecasting rapid annual growth of the internet. The report noted that web usage was growing at 2,300 percent per year. The idea of building an online bookstore with millions of titles was exciting to him. In a 2017 interview with his brother, Mark, at the Summit LA conference, Bezos said a fear of regret later in life is what motivated him the most. He said, "I don't want to be eighty years old and in a quiet moment of reflection, thinking back over my life and cataloging a bunch of major regrets." So, he quit his job, packed up, and drove cross-country to Seattle where he and five employees began developing an online bookstore. One year later, in July 1995, Bezos formally launched Amazon.com.[3]

When Bezos was telling people back then, "This is what I want to do," a lot of them probably tried to discourage him from taking that route. Keep in mind that in 1994, the concept of an online business was something you had to explain to other people. No one really knew the potential the internet had to change everything from personal communication to shopping to finding information. Jeff Bezos saw that potential, but he took a huge risk by giving up his well-paying job.

3. RESILIENCE

One definition of *resilience* is "the ability to recover from or adjust easily to misfortune or change." This is a critical trait of leaders in today's constantly changing environment. Resilience and risk-taking are somewhat correlated because when you take a risk, many times, you'll fail. A true leader gets more motivated every time he or she fails. If failure causes you to lose your motivation and give up, then that's not a trait of leadership.

Failure is so valuable to learning, in fact, that Columbia University in New York has established a new research center that is committed to figuring out how to turn failure into success.

In 2016, cognitive-studies researcher Xiaodong Lin-Siegler of Columbia University's Teachers College published a study revealing that high-school students' science grades improved after they learned about the personal and intellectual *struggles* of scientists including Albert Einstein and Marie Curie. Students who only learned about the scientists' *achievements* saw their grades decline. In April 2018, the Teachers College announced the creation of the interdisciplinary Education for Persistence and Innovation Center, which is dedicated to studying failure's educational purpose. Lin-Siegler, who is overseeing the center, is expanding her own research into the failures of successful people, starting by interviewing Nobel laureates. The center will convene researchers from various academic fields and countries in an effort to better understand how failure can facilitate learning and success.[4]

3. "Jeff Bezos Quit His Job at 30 to Launch Amazon—Here Are the 3 Simple Strategies He Used to Do It," Darren Marble, *Inc.*, October 10, 2008, https://www.inc.com/darren-marble/jeff-bezos-quit-his-job-at-30-to-launch-amazon-heres-how-to-know-if-its-right-time-for-your-big-move.html.

4. "The Value of Failing," Isabel Fattal, *The Atlantic*, April 25, 2018, https://www.theatlantic.com/education/archive/2018/04/the-value-of-failing/558848/.

In the older days, if a company was not profitable, it was not considered a good company. But today, profitability is not a requirement for success. Uber Technologies is a great example of a company we tend to consider successful. The ride-hailing company doesn't have its own inventory of vehicles, and it doesn't hire drivers as employees. Yet Uber is far from profitable.

In August 2018, Uber reported that it had narrowed losses by $1.1 billion from a year earlier. Uber's net loss was $891 million on June 30, 2018. That is a huge net loss, but still, it's a big improvement from the $1.1 billion loss from a year earlier.[5]

As mentioned in Chapter 1, Mark Zuckerberg and his college roommate and fellow Harvard University student Eduardo Saverin launched the social-networking service Facebook on February 4, 2004. In September 2009, Facebook reported that it had turned cash-flow positive for the first time.[6] The company filed for an IPO in 2012.[7]

Many companies struggle to become profitable for years and finally do so because their leaders are resilient. They do not lose motivation when they fail to reach their goals.

Other classic leaders who demonstrated great resilience include Walt Disney, Thomas Edison, and Abraham Lincoln. More contemporary leaders who are extremely resilient include Michael Jordan, Jack Ma, J. K. Rowling, Oprah Winfrey, and Tyler Perry.

A more recent example of how resilience pays off significantly is Chinese internet tycoon Jack Ma. When Ma was starting his career, he reportedly got rejected by dozens of employers, among them Kentucky Fried Chicken, which had recently entered China at the time. He later went on to become China's richest person, founding e-commerce giant Alibaba. Now Alibaba's financial affiliate, Ant Financial, will become part owner of KFC in China through an investment in Yum China.[8]

It has been said that success is the best form of revenge, and what great revenge Jack Ma got—he purchased part of the company that rejected him years earlier!

Alibaba's 2014 IPO in New York set a record as the world's biggest public stock offering, raising $25 billion. As of mid-July 2021, *Forbes* estimated Ma's net worth at $43.5 billion.[9]

Jack Ma is wildly successful now because he overcame failures with resilience.

Look at your own life. How many times have you failed and not given up? Take a moment to think about three situations when difficulties made your path challenging, but you persevered. Chances are, you went on to achieve something significant. Had you given up, you would not have achieved anything.

---

5. "Uber Narrows Loss but Still a Long Way from Profitability," Heather Somerville, Reuters, August 15, 2018, https://www.reuters.com/article/uber-results/uber-narrows-loss-but-still-a-long-way-from-profitability-idUSL1N1V611I.
6. "Facebook 'Cash Flow Positive,' Signs 300M Users," *CBC News (Canada)*, September 16, 2009, https://www.cbc.ca/news/technology/facebook-cash-flow-positive-signs-300m-users-1.826223.
7. US Securities and Exchange Commission, Form S-1, "Registration Statement: Facebook, Inc.," February 1, 2012, https://www.sec.gov/Archives/edgar/data/1326801/000119312512034517/d287954ds1.htm.
8. "Jack Ma, Rejected for Job at KFC, Buys Piece of It Instead," Jacky Wong, September 2, 2016, *The Wall Street Journal*, https://www.wsj.com/articles/BL-MBB-53019.
9. #26 Jack Ma, Forbes, July 15, 2021, https://www.forbes.com/profile/jack-ma/?sh=1a57bf01ee43.

4. CONCERN FOR OTHERS

It seems that many leaders are motivated by money, not by caring for, or being concerned about, others. But leaders lead people, and whenever people are involved, they have to be your first priority, whether they are your employees, your customers, or your investors. People are the most important asset any organization has.

How do you put others first? How do you become caring? Caring means letting other people know that what is important to them is also important to you. You demonstrate that you care by aligning their priorities with yours, meeting them at their level, and understanding why they are doing things they are doing.

Now, caring doesn't mean you give away everything people ask for, but you do need to be compassionate. You can be firm and polite at the same time. It starts with showing people that you are genuinely interested in them. When you speak with them, listen carefully. Look at them and look in their eyes, or camera on your screen if you are meeting through a virtual platform. It is quite rude to listen to people or talk to people while looking at your phone or elsewhere. Ask questions. Don't fake it, mean it and mean it well. Show that you understand.

Caring doesn't mean you have to become someone's best friend. It's OK if you don't go to their parties. It's OK if you miss their wedding. But don't miss a funeral in their family. That shows how caring you are. They should—it's not that you should say that you're caring.

Every leader goes through good times and bad times. People will remain loyal to respected leaders, even during hardships. But average or poor leaders are left with no one during the bad times. If you go out of your way to help others, they will do the same for you. They will come through for you during difficult times because you cared about them when they were struggling. People are led through "Love" and "Fear." In some cases, fear is more effective but only for short term and most usually brings disloyalty. Leading through love gives more shelf life to loyalty and gets you in the express lane of "leaving your legacy."

Treat people as you would like to be treated! Not only is it "the Golden Rule" but it also is a hallmark of leadership.

5. TRANSPARENCY IN COMMUNICATION

It's critical to be a transparent communicator, especially during challenging times. The more difficult a situation, the more important it is to be transparent. Appearing to keep important details from the people you lead will erode trust quickly.

If you are a leader, people will ask for things. It might be tempting to say to them, "Well, let me think about it," even though you have no intentions of thinking about it or doing anything about it. If someone asks you for a raise and you have no intention of giving that person a raise, communicate that, and tell the person why. If you say you will think about it, that gives the person false hope. And when the person finally discovers that no raise is in your plans, he or she will be disappointed and will feel worse than if you had been open and honest upon the first request.

It's OK to give someone bad news, as long as you're very transparent. Do this consistently to build a reputation as an honest leader. When you do that, people will begin to take you for your word. People like leaders who do what they say they will do and who give them honest insight into what is really happening.

People don't want to hear about a major development in the organization from someone else. Often, we read about a company that is laying off people and having an outside firm break the news to employees. This shows a lack of respect for the people who work for you.

Imagine that a friend of yours asks you if you will lend him some money. He promises you that he will repay the money in one week. The next week comes, and your friend is nowhere to be found. You try to call or visit him, but he is avoiding you. Three months later, he finally pays you back. This changes your perception about him, doesn't it?

It would have been better if he had told you in person, face to face, "I know I was supposed to give you the money back this week, but I am unable to do so, and here is the reason."

We are naturally trained to avoid conflict and don't like to tell people what they want to hear. We often forget that the transparency eventually comes out, through you or otherwise; it is worst if it is not delivered through you in a timely manner. Transparent communication will always earn you respect in the long run.

6. CONFIDENCE

Confidence is a trait that makes it much easier to communicate with transparency. When leaders are confident, people feel they can trust them.

Imagine that you are sitting in a commercial airplane, flying from New York to Chicago; the weather is inclement and just as the plane is about to land in Chicago, it takes off again. The plane begins to shake, and the crew members start to panic. The pilot does not explain over the intercom what is happening. Now all the passengers are murmuring, discussing with one another what might be happening. Panic sets in, and people are certain the plane is going to crash. They think and say, "Something is wrong! Why didn't the plane land? Why did the plane almost land and then take off again? Why are the flight attendants panicking? Why isn't the pilot communicating with us?"

Now, let's imagine that the same situation happens, but this time, the pilot's voice comes over the intercom and says, "Folks, just as we were about to land in Chicago, we lost our spot because another flight was delayed. So, we had to ascend again, and it's going to be shaky up here for a little while. We'll probably be up in the air for the next fifteen minutes. Keep your seatbelts fastened, and don't worry. We'll get you down safely just as soon as we can."

That is clear, confident communication. Nothing has changed—the plane is still shaking, and the crew is still running around. What did change is that a confident leader communicated with you. Now everyone understands what is happening and can relax.

Everyone went about going to their own things and you forgot about that shaking part. It's critical for us to appear confident because people expect things from the leader.

If your CEO announces that your company is laying people off and communicates that he is doing everything possible to change that outcome or to find everyone new jobs, people will gain confidence in that leader. People expect their leaders to be confident. The leader's confidence serves as the fuel for their followers.

Communicating bad news with confidence is more effective than sharing good news without confidence.

7. INTUITION

Another trait of leadership is intuition. One definition of ***intuition*** is "the power or faculty of attaining to direct knowledge or cognition without evident rational thought and inference." I believe intuition cannot be learned; you either have it, or you don't.

Intuition is a gift that many people don't have. If you have this trait and don't use it to improve your organization and the world around you, it's a shame. Intuition is seeing things that many other people cannot see. Leaders who have intuition are visionary leaders.

I believe I have some traces of intuition. But I didn't realize it until I started my own business. Once I began to tap into my intuition, I looked back at my failures and realized that I could have avoided them if I had just trusted my intuition. I believe that many of my successes have been a combination of intuition, luck, and maybe my mother sending me positive vibes from heaven.

How do you know if you are gifted with intuition? Some people in the world are blessed with intuition yet they are not able to fully leverage it to their potential. Many of us grew up with an uncle or aunt in our family who was intuitive and well respected in the family for their foresight. They may have earned the reputation of being the "wise person" by providing iniutitive contributions, though they may have not changed the world. Not every intuitive person has to change the world, but it is a rare talent and those who are willing and able to make a difference should have the opportunity to do so.

Go back to your uninfluenced decisions in life. Have you been right when others disagreed with you? Is there a pattern of your forward thinking and your gut feeling proving you right, even when most disagreed with you? In that case, you have the gift of intuition, and you still may have time to benefit from this gift. Always being right about the ripeness of a watermelon may not qualify you as intuitive. Also, predicting the stock market correctly a few times is too risky to certify you as intuitive. You may very well be, but this is one risk I can't advise you to take regularly.

8. THE ABILITY TO INSPIRE OTHERS

Being inspiring is not just an important trait for leaders; managers should be inspiring as well. People who have entered management after being in sales or in other roles soon discover that they need an entirely different skill set to lead a team.

Most of us are skilled at motivating ourselves to do something, but it takes a lot of skill to inspire other people to achieve high levels of performance on their own. It requires that you bring out the best in them so that they can generate intrinsic, or internal, motivation to accomplish a goal.

Most great leaders are so good at inspiring others that they create armies of loyal followers. When people respect and appreciate their leaders, they will push themselves to much greater levels of performance than they will simply for a monetary benefit.

This is true in sports as well as in business. When you have a favorite sports team or favorite athletes, you follow them and admire them. The way they play inspires you. When they win, you don't make money (unless you were placing bets on the final score), but it makes you happy. And when your team or athlete loses, it can ruin your whole day. You didn't lose anything personally, but you still felt bad. For passionate sports fans, no other feelings can match the joy you get when your team wins the championship.

This is true of political, religious, and business leaders, too. If you have the ability to inspire others, you can accomplish much more than you can on your own.

I believe you can learn how to be inspiring by taking specialized leadership training courses. It also requires that you get to know every person on your team. Find out what is important to them, what they fear, what they hope for, and what they want to accomplish. There is no greater reward than helping people see what is possible, helping them recognize their own gifts, and taking them to places they cannot go on their own. When people see that you are doing that for them, they will feel inspired by you.

Nelson Mandela was an extremely inspiring person. He showed an entire nation, South Africa, that apartheid could be eliminated. He took his nation to a place where they could not go on their own. Leaders without the ability to inspire others end up incentivizing through other means, they are most often less effective and more expensive.

9. PATIENCE

Patience is a valuable virtue, whether you are a business leader, a parent, a coach, a teacher, a nurse, a retail clerk, a bus driver … everyone needs patience. People who react with anger when they don't get their way immediately are immature. People who demand immediate results can appear immature.

Because of advances in technology, we have come to expect immediate gratification. But sometimes immediate results are not possible, and great leaders always demonstrate patience. Trying to employ quick fixes to big problems can make things worse. When you address situations calmly and patiently, it shows wisdom and maturity. People will view you as a wise, knowledgeable, thoughtful leader.

Patience is a great vaccine for anger.

Not all leaders are gifted with patience. People, and the business environment, often expect results immediately. Many dynamic leaders do not have patience, which is a weakness, in my view. However, many consider a lack of patience as their strength. I believe that patience in not gender-biased, people can be impatient. Some men wrongfully expect women to be more patient. Patience is a triat that leaders need, regardless of their gender.

10. SELF-CONTROL

A lack of self-control often becomes the primary reason for a "fall from grace" for accomplished leaders. I believe the two most common reasons for an abrupt end of leadership are ill-health and a lack of self-control. Your health, to a great extent, is not fully in your control.

However, sometimes ill-health is the result of a lack of self-control—engaging in unhealthy behaviors or leaving addictions unaddressed. Leaders can help sustain their health by adapting a healthy lifestyle. It is important for leaders to be in good health. A sick leader is always a temporary leader. Here are some critical factors for improving health and wellness:

1. Sleep well (eight hours) and start your day early.
2. Eat well.
3. Exercise and monitor your health regularly.
4. Maintain work–life balance.
5. Keep a positive attitude.

History is witness to numerous unceremonious ends of erstwhile great leaders. Richard Nixon, Tiger Woods, Lance Armstrong, O. J. Simpson, Bill Cosby, Harvey Weinstein, Travis Kalanick, and many more could have been great leaders in their fields, but they are likely to be remembered instead for their "falls from grace." All of these leaders lacked self-control, which led to poor judgment, and their lifetime work was overshadowed by a claim to shame.

Lack of self-control can convert an accomplished leader into a wimp. Leaders must demonstrate extreme discipline to exert self-control. At times, health is not always in our control, but self-control is.

11. INTEGRITY

Integrity is firm adherence to a code of moral values. You either have integrity or you don't. It's a part of your ethical upbringing.

Leaders with integrity never announce their integrity; it is the other way around.

Many of us learn integrity from our grandmothers. Integrity measures how committed you are to doing what's right. It is believing in, and acting by, the right values. Today, we have a culture that often does not reward integrity. Many entrepreneurs make a lot of money but would not score very high on integrity. If you want to be an effective, trusted leader, integrity is one of the most important elements to embrace. History will not be kind to you if you have demonstrated the other leadership traits but fail to have integrity.

To me, integrity is the core, the foundation, of leadership. Integrity is always expensive in the short term and valuable in the long term.

Many leaders find integrity easy to preach but hard to practice. Leaders with integrity are leaders of principle. As a leader, you often come across a situation in which integrity comes with a high cost. If you are faced with a situation where you need to evaluate your benefits for exercising integrity, then you need to bolster your integrity. A person with integrity does not spend any time deciding about integrity. It is who he or she is.

12. THE ABILITY TO DELEGATE

Great leaders are effective at delegating work to the people around them who are most qualified to handle specific tasks. There is a finite number of hours in every day, and you cannot do everything yourself. Leaders spend their time doing the types of work no one else can do, and they delegate the rest.

Leaders do not do everything on their own. They also do not sit down and create PowerPoint presentations or update their websites. Instead, they surround themselves with talented people who excel in all different types of tasks. Good delegation means identifying the right talent, preparing those people to do what needs to be done, and matching the assignment to the talent.

Hire the right people, coach them, and let them do the work.

In a nutshell, a leader's job is to do the following:

1. Attract, retain, and groom the best talent.
2. Coach them.
3. Open doors for them when they hit a wall.
4. Regularly provide feedback and guidance.

SUCCESS DOES NOT EQUAL GREATNESS

Can someone be successful without possessing these twelve traits of leaders? Yes. But success does not equal greatness. Someone who is resilient and patient might not have integrity, so even though that person might be wealthy, most people would not consider him or her a true leader.

As leaders, it is our responsibility to strengthen these leadership traits so we can lead others more effectively. That is how we will fulfill our potential and help others fulfill their potential. To accomplish this, you must be willing, able, and allowed to do so.

There are many prospective leaders who want to become leaders and had the ability to do so. However, they are not allowed to become leaders. Also, there are many leaders who have the ability and opportunity to be leaders, but not the willingness or desire. Both ability and desire to be a leader are necessary elements of a future in leadership.

Last, we all know of some lucky people who had the willingness and the opportunity to become leaders, yet their leadership rodeo was short-lived, primarily due to a lack of ability. If you want to be a leader, strengthen these traits. Be aware of your strengths and weaknesses and be prepared to create the opportunity to lead.

To determine whether leadership is an appropriate calling for you, ask yourself, "What is my goal in life?" If you have all the traits or many of the traits of leadership, yet you have no desire to be a leader, you should never force yourself to be a leader.

Success is common and self-defined to an extent; greatness is rare and always defined by history.

There is great responsibility and great reward in being a leader. Accomplishing something great on your own is somewhat fulfilling, but imagine that you impact hundreds, thousands, or more people in a positive way. There is nothing more fulfilling than that, in my opinion.

Most leaders want to be remembered as great leaders. However, only few can become great. Greatness is simple but not easy. If you want to be great, then do something that will have an impact on the people and the society over a long period of time. It is not about money, fame, or power; it is not even about the leader as an individual. Greatness is about the change that leaders bring about by improving society. Greatness is never self-acclaimed; that is an illusion. Let history make a call on this.

THREE TRAITS LEADERS NEED IN CHANGING TIMES

The twelve traits I just listed were important traits of leadership in the past, and they are still important today. But leadership in changing times requires some additional traits.

1. FLEXIBILITY

Millennials, who are in the workforce now, and Gen Z, who will enter the workforce soon, have different rules of engagement than previous generations. These younger generations have grown up in an era of unprecedented technological change. They are flexible and adaptable by nature. They are "digital natives" who may not know about things as their previous generations did; however, they know how to use technology to get things done.

Those of us who did not grow up with today's technology need to learn how to adapt quickly as technology changes the reality of our everyday lives. Young people today are driven by technology; they don't know what it's like to be without a smartphone or social media. They prefer to communicate differently than the ways we might prefer. We must adapt to changing times if we want to lead others effectively. It's impossible to be viewed as an effective leader if we can't even keep up with our younger colleagues' communication methods.

We must learn how to stay relevant in changing times. This might mean we have to learn from younger people. We might need to take classes in optimizing social media marketing opportunities or in creating digital training. We cannot continue to do things the way we always have and hope to connect with younger people in the workforce.

2. WILLINGNESS TO EMBRACE INCLUSION AND DIVERSITY

When I was starting my career, the boss was always older than the workforce, and he was usually a male. Leaders were father figures. There were few female leaders and no younger leaders. But all of that is changing now.

Most of us may eventually work for someone who is younger and female.

A few years ago, I was asked to do a television interview in Manhattan. The TV station sent a limousine from a private company to pick me up. The driver was running late, and I could tell by the way he was driving that he did not know his way around.

I asked him, "Are you a new driver?"

He said, "Yeah. I just started about two weeks ago."

I gave him some directions and tips on how to avoid traffic. As he drove, I asked him what type of work he had done previously.

He replied, "I had a very good job. I was a manager at a Starbucks store."

I asked him what happened—why he was no longer working there. He said, "I loved my job. I was very happy there. Then all of a sudden, they decided to bring in a new regional vice president who was a woman." He paused and then added, "I cannot work for a woman."

When I asked him what he meant by that, he said, "I cannot take orders from a woman, and she did not know what she was doing. I just couldn't take it. So, I quit."

I asked the driver, "Was she not nice to you?"

He said she was nice enough.

Then I asked him, "Did you make up your mind before you interacted with her that you would not work with her?"

He said yes, and I told him I was a marketing researcher and wanted to learn more about it. I asked him if something happened that made him believe that women failed as leaders.

He said, "No. Please don't misunderstand me. I love my wife and my daughter, and I respect them very much, but I cannot imagine taking orders from a woman. I am the man in my household. I bring home the bacon. I serve as the leader in my house. I see that as a great role and an important role."

I asked him, "Is your daughter going to school?"

"Yeah. She's very smart. She's young."

I said, "One day, she's going to attend college. And then she will work."

He agreed, and I asked him, "What message do you have for people who will work for her? Do you think she will lead a team that is full of women only?"

He said, "No, no, no. I hope that doesn't happen. But I cannot change myself."

He was being honest. Even today, this is a mindset that many people have. This man had an unconscious bias, and it became a conscious bias.

We are living in an environment in which many of us have unconscious biases that will become a challenge for new leaders who are not as likely to have such biases. It will be difficult for younger leaders to manage people who resist the natural order of our changing demographics. They have never lived in a world in which all the leaders were older white males in the western world and mostly males in the rest of the world.

Today, women, millennials, and people from multicultural backgrounds compose seventy-six percent of the U.S. population. Today, diversity is the norm. Leaders today need to face their biases and fears about working with people different from themselves. They cannot lead effectively unless they embrace people from different backgrounds and create an environment of inclusion.

Leaders should be known by their ability to inspire others to greatness. They should not be known by their gender, age, race, ethnicity, religion, or sexual orientation. I believe younger leaders are better prepared to lead diverse teams.

Many people resisted the internet and social media when they became commonplace, and eventually, they learned to appreciate the benefits these technological advances offer. The same is true of diversity. Many people, like the limo driver, resist embracing diversity. But once people begin to see how rich and robust our society can become when we include everyone, they will hopefully begin to appreciate people who came from backgrounds different from their own.

It's not enough just to accept diversity; leaders must embrace diversity and practice inclusion. Accepting something means that you are resigned to living with something because it is a reality or a requirement. It's like going to the dentist. You don't enjoy getting a root canal, but you have to, or you will experience pain and lose your tooth. But embracing something means you are happy that things are changing, and you see the benefits.

3. A COMMITMENT TO A SUSTAINABLE ENVIRONMENT

We used to print all our documents without thinking about our actions affected the environment. We used to mail out printed newsletters, get our bank statements in the mail, and mail our annual reports to stakeholders. But today, we are living in an environment in which we are more conscious of our need to leave this world as a better place for the next generation. We need to conserve water and protect the environment.

Leaders cannot ignore this responsibility.

When your bank, utility service, or credit-card company sends you a request to switch to online billing, do you sign up for it? Or do you continue to receive your bills and statements in the mail?

I do not believe it is possible to be a responsible, forward-thinking leader without acknowledging the need for, and contributing to, environmental change. We all need to look at our processes and systems and make changes to preserve our environment. Leaders are responsible for creating the sustainable environment.

Now it's time for a self-assessment. What leadership traits do you have, and how strong are they? Which traits would you like to improve? Rate yourself on the following scale, with 1 being weak and 10 being strong. Commit to strengthening those traits you feel are weaker. Imagine how much you can impact other people's lives by making the most of your leadership potential.

LEADERSHIP TRAITS SELF-ASSESSMENT

Innovative vision:

1 2 3 4 5 6 7 8 9 10

A risk-taking mentality:

1 2 3 4 5 6 7 8 9 10

Resilience:

1 2 3 4 5 6 7 8 9 10

Level of concern for others:

1 2 3 4 5 6 7 8 9 10

Transparency in communication:

1 2 3 4 5 6 7 8 9 10

Confidence:

1 2 3 4 5 6 7 8 9 10

Effectiveness at delegating:

1 2 3 4 5 6 7 8 9 10

Intuition:

1 2 3 4 5 6 7 8 9 10

The ability to inspire others:

1 2 3 4 5 6 7 8 9 10

Patience:

1 2 3 4 5 6 7 8 9 10

Self-control:

1 2 3 4 5 6 7 8 9 10

Integrity:

1 2 3 4 5 6 7 8 9 10

The ability to delegate:

1 2 3 4 5 6 7 8 9 10

Flexibility:

1 2 3 4 5 6 7 8 9 10

Willingness to embrace diversity and inclusion:

1 2 3 4 5 6 7 8 9 10

A commitment to a sustainable environment:

1 2 3 4 5 6 7 8 9 10

SUMMARY

- Leaders create opportunities for others, find the most talented person for each role, and inspire others to achieve greatness.
- Integrity is essential to being an effective leader.
- Not everyone who has leadership traits wants to be a leader. It should not be forced; both ability and desire to be a leader are necessary elements of a future in leadership.
- There is nothing more fulfilling than impacting hundreds, thousands, or more people in a positive way.

QUOTES BY TARIQ KHAN

One of the most important things for a leader is good health. Some great leaders succumbed to health helplessly.

Good leaders challenge people, great leaders challenge the system.

CHAPTER 5

Leaders versus Managers—Understanding the Differences and Working Together

CHAPTER LEARNING OBJECTIVES

1. Learn why entrepreneurs need good managers on their teams, and vice versa.
2. Examine nine traits that differentiate leaders from managers.
3. Complete a self-assessment to determine if you are more of a leader or manager.

I want to be very clear about one fact: both managers and leaders are critical in any organization. I have seen many organizations run without a leader for a short term, but I have never seen any organization run without a manager. They are both critical assets of any organization, any entity, but they are very distinct in their approach, mindset, responsibility, and expectations.

An entrepreneur is a unique breed of leader. In general, managers should manage, and leaders should lead. But entrepreneurship pretty much forces you to be a manager *and* a leader at the same time. Especially if it's an early-stage company, you're not in a position to hire a team of managers.

In the morning, when you get to the office, or if you're working from your garage or your basement, you are a manager. You are handling the day-to-day aspects of the business. Then, when you're taking a shower, you're probably thinking about big-picture aspects of your business, your vision—which is what a leader does. If you are like me, does all your great ideas come to you when you are in the shower of driving. Start recording your showers (voice only) and delete them once you capture them.

NOT ALL MANAGERS RISE TO LEADERSHIP

Before people become leaders, they are sometimes managers. I've seen many good managers become good leaders. That's a natural progression for many. But once you become a leader, you cannot resume being a manager. Once you assume the role of a leader, it becomes challenging for you to be in a managerial role. That's why many entrepreneurs fail—they try to be both the leader and the manager because they don't like to invest in managers. They try to fulfill both roles at once, and that is typically not an effective approach.

I have seen many people move up the ranks to leadership because they knew how to manage up within an organization, but they always had the mindset of a manager. They couldn't give up the daily management tasks. Leaders in large- and mid-size companies usually have to report to a board of directors. Once you reach that stage, you need to delegate the nuts-and-bolts decisions to other people. Leaders need to resist the urge to do everything on their own.

If you micromanage your staff members and ask for details, you are still managing–not leading.

Ideally, a person who is being considered for a leadership role will receive training in the skills that are specific to that type of role. It requires different skill set to be an effective leader than it does to be an effective manager. Unfortunately, too many managers are rushed into leadership with no training and expected to learn on the job. That can work if the person has an innate set of leadership skills, but often, situations like that do not turn out well.

Good leaders rely on their managers to remain their loyal partners for the long term. Great leaders prepare their managers for leadership if those managers have the aptitude and desire for that role.

EXPERIENCE DESERVES RESPECT; SO DO ENTREPRENEURS

When I was twenty-five, I didn't see the value in a person's professional experience. When older people would talk about their experience, it didn't mean anything to me. I didn't take it seriously. But now I'm at that age where I realize how naïve I was that I didn't value experience.

But today, I see young, dynamic leaders who are successful entrepreneurs, and although they might not say it, I don't think they have much respect for people who are experienced leaders. I sometimes see on Twitter that young leaders get into tweeting competitions with older leaders. These young, successful people have accomplished some great things, but still, I think there is no replacement for experience, which comes over time. At the very least, we should appreciate, acknowledge, and respect people's lifetime experience.

Now, the life cycle of entrepreneurship is much shorter than the classic leadership model. People launch innovative companies while very young and often get rejected early in their careers, unless they inherit a business from family members or someone else. They are getting high-level business experience that young people didn't typically get in the past. But still, wisdom comes with age, if it ever does, and young people cannot possibly gain the same valuable wisdom that someone much older has earned simply by experiencing many different economic and political cycles, world events, and changing life stages.

Young entrepreneurs who are visionaries would be wise to understand that they need to hire competent managers who can bring their dreams to fruition. Hire a manager who is a lot more experienced than you and a lot more mature than you.

Also, give respect to every entrepreneur. Most entrepreneurs can possibly find higher paying jobs at large companies with fancy titles. They are mission driven and committed to fill a gap, create a product, or change the world. Yes, many may fail again and again in doing that, yet they choose a riskier path for a more rewarding career—and then some.

I have often seen some corporate officers to unnecessarily play "hard to connect" with entrepreneurs or small-business owners. Please treat them fairly because they, too, have earned bragging rights to be entrepreneurs. They have taken a huge risk to start their own businesses. Most people do well while working for companies, whereas others do well while working for themselves. Very few people are gifted to do both well.

One time, I was speaking at a conference at Harvard University. The room was almost full of more than two hundred bright students. One young lady stood up and asked me this question: "In my career, I have worked for companies, and now, I work for myself. What is the difference?"

I replied, "When you work for a company, your compensation is guaranteed, but your job is not. When you work for yourself, your job is guaranteed, but your compensation is not."

Those entrepreneurs who step out and take the risk to work for themselves and experience erratic compensation—or even none at times—earn the respect they deserve.

MANY ENTREPRENEURS SKIP THE TRADITIONAL CAREER PATH

Back in the 1980s and 1990s, there was a standard career path most people were expected to follow. You started out in sales, and if your boss saw that you had management potential, he (it was usually a man) would invest in training you to become a manager. There was no direct entry point to become a leader. If you wanted to be the CEO of a company, your best bet was to play the politics correctly, or maybe rise through the ranks because you were related to the company's founders.

Back then, it was unheard of for young, inexperienced people to go out and launch companies like Alibaba, Amazon, Apple, Facebook, Google, Instagram, Tesla, Uber, and YouTube. But today, young visionaries skip the career path and find venture capitalists to fund their start-up companies. Most of these companies have experienced dramatic growth in short periods of time.

In the older days, the only source of financing was a bank. And banks would give you money for your idea only if you could prove to them that you *did not need* the money. It was difficult for companies to launch and grow. The companies that have been around for more than fifty years were built on a traditional, classic growth model.

Venture capitalists created a new business model. If they invest in twenty start-ups and one of them becomes successful, it will pay for the money they invested in the other nineteen companies. Money became cheap.

But there has been a serious preparation gap in the successful launch of many of today's successful companies. Many of the leaders who are doing very well with these companies were not very well prepared.

UBER'S FOUNDERS EXPERIENCED BOTH SUCCESS AND FAILURE

When ride-hailing company Uber was founded, the idea caught on and attracted a huge following. But because the company's founders were not well versed in leadership, the company experienced some serious problems.

In 2008, two friends, Travis Kalanick and Garrett Camp, were attending LeWeb, an annual tech conference in Paris. When they were unable to get a cab, they came up with the idea for a timeshare limo service that could be ordered via an app. In 2011, Uber raised a $11 million Series A round of funding led by Benchmark Capital and expanded its service to more cities. Then Uber raised $37 million in Series B funding from Menlo Ventures, Jeff Bezos, and Goldman Sachs. In 2016, Uber raised $3.5 billion from Saudi Arabia's Wealth Fund.[1]

In April 2017, Uber reported a global loss of $3.8 billion for 2016. Uber faced fierce opposition from the taxi industry and government regulators and then began to experience competition from Lyft. In June 2017, Kalanick resigned after a shareholder revolt. A former female Uber engineer claimed the company operated a sexist culture in a 3,000-word blog post. Uber's board called for an internal investigation, which became known as the "Holder Investigation" because it was led by former Attorney General Eric Holder. About two months later, Dara Khosrowshahi, who was the CEO of Expedia, took over the leadership of Uber. Khosrowshahi had come to New York in 1978 with his parents to escape the Iranian revolution.[2]

Uber's founders, Kalanick and Camp, were visionaries and did very well, but as you can see, they experienced serious problems with profitability and culture. They were typical entrepreneurs who were not charged with making the company profitable. And that's OK; profit doesn't have to be the primary goal initially, but eventually, the investors have to recoup their investment.

Uber still has not made a profit. According to *New York* magazine, "No ultimately successful major technology company has been as deeply unprofitable for anywhere remotely as long as Uber has been. After nine years, Uber isn't within hailing distance of making money and continues to bleed more red ink than any start-up in history. By contrast, Facebook and Amazon were solidly cash-flow positive by their fifth year."[3]

1. "The Story of Uber," Dan Blystone, Investopedia, August 9, 2018, https://www.investopedia.com/articles/personal-finance/111015/story-uber.asp.
2. Ibid.
3. "Uber Is Headed for a Crash," Yves Smith, *New York Magazine*, December 4, 2018, http://nymag.com/intelligencer/2018/12/will-uber-survive-the-next-decade.html.

Companies can make a profit, and/or they can have value. Although Uber has not always been profitable, it is a valuable company. So how can a company that is losing money seek an initial public offering with a valuation of $120 billion?

It's because Uber has created a niche, a market, a customer base, and a model that can be replicated but not duplicated. The company has created a desire and a need for its service. Before Uber came into the marketplace, nobody was asking for a transportation service that had no vehicle fleet of its own but rather relied on hired drivers who used their own vehicles. In a similar way, when Steve Jobs invented the iPad, he created the need and desire for a product people never even knew about previously.

Most entrepreneurs create innovative solutions for existing problems.

Disruptive entrepreneurs first create the problem we don't have and then find a solution for it.

TECHNOLOGY PROVIDES THE ILLUSION OF CONTROL

In the older days, if I needed to develop a manager, I had to have eye-to-eye contact with that person and spend time coaching him or her. But today, some of my best managers are people who live far away from where I live; in fact, I have never met some of them in person.

Technology has opened up the boundaries. Today there are no geographical boundaries as we create global teams who work seamlessly in different locations.

But how can we develop, manage, and lead people when you aren't in the same room with them, and your team members are in several different time zones, scattered around the world? Working with remote teams is a challenge for leaders and managers alike.

When I was a kid, my parents were very happy when I was home because they knew I couldn't get in trouble if I was home. They could watch me. But that isn't true today. You could be sitting in the same room as your eleven-year-old daughter. You might think she is doing her homework or chatting with a friend, but she could be interacting with a seventy-year-old man in a different continent who is pretending to be her age. Or she could be navigating websites she shouldn't be visiting. You have the illusion of being in control of the situation because your daughter or son is there with you, but technology has presented significant dangers.

Fifteen years ago, I remember not being allowed to visit social media websites while at work. We could not log in to Facebook or bring an Apple device to work. Why? Because companies wanted to remain in control. But control is an illusion. Today, when I teach at NYU, I am standing in front of twenty-five students who are sitting there with their digital devices. I might say, "Hey, pay attention. I'm talking."

And they'll say, "Yeah. We're listening to you and making notes."

But in my classrooms today, I see no paper notebooks.

They might be taking notes, but how do I know that they're not navigating on Instagram or some other site?

This fact is upsetting to many people who feel like they have lost the ability to control what happens in their work environment. But the truth is, if you have to watch people that closely, something is wrong. If you feel like you have to monitor their search histories on their computers, that is not an effective use of your time.

Instead, discuss the work that needs to be done and ensure that people understand what you expect of them and by when. That's it.

Someday, when we have to start managing and leading robots, the rules of engagement will change even more drastically.

LEADERS RECOGNIZE WHEN THEY ARE DISTRACTED

When the New Year arrived in 2019, I made a resolution to go on a "social media diet."

I looked at the analytics on my phone. I saw that, on average, I was spending forty-two to fifty hours per week on my phone. That's a full-time work week. I did a detailed analysis to find out exactly how I was spending my time on my phone.

Social media ate up the biggest chunk of time, followed by reading and productivity tasks. My social media time increased on the weekends; I was spending six to eight hours each weekend day on social media. I like to stay up late, and around midnight, I was spending an hour to an hour and a half on my phone, visiting social media sites watching videos just for fun. Those were valuable hours that I needed to sleep, so I was not using my time productively. I had not realized how much social media was distracting me from more important leadership tasks.

My smartphone is also my learning tool; I post and read blogs on it. So, some of the time I spend on my phone is benefiting me; I am educating myself. But it's easy to get sidetracked. I know I need to drive the technology and avoid letting the technology drive me. I think that's an important question we all need to ask ourselves: "Am I controlling my device, or is it controlling me?"

Therefore, I decided to go on a social media diet. I am going to spend less time on social media and more time with people in my life, having face-to-face conversations with them. I don't want to have lunches and dinners with everyone looking at their phones and still trying to carry on a conversation. Some people might think they're multitasking, but I see that as ignoring the people at the table.

To me, it is insulting if I am trying to coach or mentor someone who is looking down at a phone and saying, "Yeah, I got you." Technology has given us powerful tools that can be valuable and productive, but we need to use them to our advantage, not to our disadvantage.

NINE TRAITS THAT DIFFERENTIATE LEADERS FROM MANAGERS

The following is a list of differences between leaders and managers. Once again, I want to emphasize that one role is not better than the other. Both are important pillars of an organization, but the roles require different responsibilities. At the end of this section is a checklist you can use to assess yourself in these areas.

1. A LEADER IS AN INNOVATOR; A MANAGER IS AN IMPLEMENTER

A leader looks to the future and envisions what the organization could be like. He or she establishes a vision. In contrast, a manager ensures that the vision becomes a reality; he or she executes the vision.

Leaders want to take their team members to places they cannot get to on their own. They're always thinking about ideas that other people might consider to be unrealistic. But innovation is in the DNA of leaders. They want to create something new. They don't like to follow; they like to lead. Leaders don't want to be told how someone else did something. A true leader always innovates on his or her own terms.

Now, managers are good at implementing visions and ideas. They are skilled at executing the idea the leader has and making it come to fruition in the way the leader envisioned it.

2. A LEADER CHALLENGES THE SYSTEM; A MANAGER MAINTAINS THE SYSTEM

Leaders tend to challenge established systems. For that reason, your result will not be ideal if you ask a leader who has challenged a system to maintain that system.

A manager will make sure that people do not deviate from whatever system is created.

A leader, by nature, is a restless soul. A leader is someone who can never predict what will happen tomorrow but knows that something will happen tomorrow. While managers help minimize surprises that can rattle team members, leaders are focused more on capitalizing on innovative new ideas.

3. A LEADER CREATES IDEAS; A MANAGER CREATES EVENTS

Leaders are always thinking about how they can create a legacy. They want to do things no one else has done, and they want to be remembered for it. In contrast, managers want to make sure things are prepared and executed at the proper time. They establish guidelines and follow them.

For example, as soon as a meeting is announced, the manager will be planning the agenda, inviting the appropriate attendees, scheduling the venue, preparing the handouts, and lining up the audiovisual team. Meanwhile, the leader is figuring out how to inspire the people who attend the meeting and challenge each one to handle their respective tasks in the optimum way.

4. A LEADER FOCUSES ON THE VISION; A MANAGER FOCUSES ON THE MISSION

A vision is a leader's view of future possibilities, whereas the mission is the process of getting there. A vision is where we want to be, and the mission is where we are. The manager is the one who executes the mission using a measurable process that has clear steps and time frames.

I believe there are far more implementers of missions than there are visionaries. If you are one of the few who is a visionary, you are fortunate. However, your vision will not be meaningful until you find people who can implement it well.

5. A LEADER DEVELOPS TALENT; A MANAGER TRAINS TALENT

Managers see the roles that need to be filled, and they hire the ideal people for those jobs and help the new hires master their jobs. But leaders are looking to prepare people for their *next* jobs. It's a different mindset. Leaders are always coaching people who can replace themselves, whereas managers focus on training people they can depend on. It's an important difference.

6. A LEADER INSPIRES; A MANAGER INSPECTS

When a leader is interacting with people, he or she describes the vision and inspires team members to want to be a part of the vision. Leaders won't set out a clear guideline on how to get there; that's where the managers come in.

Managers are very methodological about inspecting what needs to be done, by whom, and by what date. They work as partners to the leader, benchmarking progress to make sure the team is meeting critical milestones along the way. Managers are inspective by nature. They figure out if everyone is doing what they are supposed to do. Leaders are fine with deviating from the original plan, but managers see it as their job to ensure that no one deviates from the plan.

7. A LEADER TAKES RISKS; A MANAGER MANAGES RISK

Leaders take risks, and managers focus on managing risks. Leaders consider "risk" to be a positive word, whereas managers often consider "risk" to be a negative word.

Leaders look forward to navigating uncharted territory and exploring new possibilities, even if risks are involved. Meanwhile, the leaders around them are trying to control the risks.

Prolific innovator Richard Branson ignites new risks and starts new companies regularly. The people who work with him probably find it nerve-wracking to try to balance his adventuresome spirit with controlling risks and liabilities. And that's the key—there must be a balance between the two that is best achieved with a compatible entrepreneur and manager team.

8. A LEADER CREATES NEEDS; A MANAGER FULFILLS NEEDS

Leaders create needs, and managers fulfill needs. What excites leaders most is not solving existing problems but rather creating solutions to problems people didn't know they had.

Apple created iPads, and people loved them. Now, many people can't imagine living life without one. But we did not need seven models of iPads in that many years. Every time a new version comes out, people get excited and wait in line at retail stores for hours to be one of the first to get the new version. I personally don't see much difference in the various models. So, Apple has converted a want into a need. That's what a leader's job is.

Managers are very good at fulfilling those needs. When Steve Jobs created the concept for his Apple products, he didn't actually sit down and build them. No—he had a team of very skillful and successful managers and engineers who executed his vision.

9. A LEADER CREATES VALUE; A MANAGER EVALUATES VALUE

Leaders create value, and managers evaluate value. It's a different mindset, yet companies need both talents.

For example, a *leader* might decide to establish an online training portal and do away with all live workshops, seminars, and presentations. It is the *manager's* job to evaluate online training providers, compare costs and installation time frames, hire the best company, oversee the installation, train all employees on the new system, and evaluate the system's effectiveness.

Again, leadership and management are two entirely different roles, and they require different approaches, mindsets, and skills. One is not better than the other. It's simply a matter of matching a person's skill set with the role that can make the best use of those skills.

If you're not sure if your path aligns more closely with leadership or management, complete this simple exercise. In the chart below, mark where you feel your skills fall on the spectrum from the left side (management) to the right side (leadership). Then look at the completed graph. If you marked more categories toward the left side of the graph, you are likely a born manager. If you marked more categories toward the right side, you are likely a great candidate for leadership.

SELF-ASSESSMENT: ARE YOU MORE OF A MANAGER OR A LEADER?

Circle the number in each category below to indicate which of the two terms you identify with more.

1. I consider myself an…

1	2	3	4	5	6	7	8	9	10
Implementer									Innovator

2. I prefer to…

1	2	3	4	5	6	7	8	9	10
Maintain the system									Challenge the system

3. I like to…

1	2	3	4	5	6	7	8	9	10
Create events									Create ideas

4. I tend to focus on the…

1	2	3	4	5	6	7	8	9	10
Mission									Vision

5. I would rather…

1	2	3	4	5	6	7	8	9	10
Develop talent									Train talent

6. I enjoy…

1	2	3	4	5	6	7	8	9	10

Inspiring people — **Inspecting people's performance**

7. I would rather…

1	2	3	4	5	6	7	8	9	10

Take risks — **Manage risk**

8. I would prefer to…

1	2	3	4	5	6	7	8	9	10

Fulfill needs — **Create needs**

9. I am better at…

1	2	3	4	5	6	7	8	9	10

Evaluating value — **Creating value**

Look at your answers. Do you score more heavily in leadership traits or in management traits? Knowing where your interests lie will help you be more effective in your work and relationships, regardless of what that looks like.

LEADERSHIP IN A NON-PROFIT ORGANIZATION

Leadership in a non-profit sector is quite interesting and different. While it has some unique challenges, it is uniquely gratifying. I have served on several non-profit boards for nearly 20 years, and I also had the opportunity to mentor and work with many non-profit leaders. I have seen many non-profit leaders (CEO/President/Executive Director) working as managers, not leaders. In most cases, non-profit leaders are not able to manage up well and the board chairs become the functional leader.

The relationship between the leader and the board is simple but can easily get complicated. Both the functional leader and the board chair are equally responsible for creating the leadership conundrum. In my opinion, the board's role is to provide oversight, guidance, and coaching. The board should ensure to bring the most qualified person to lead the organization and then get out of their way and let them perform. The functional leader should be the face of the organization and run day-to-day operations. She/he should keep the board chair engaged and updated (monthly presidential report) on all important matters. The board or the board chair should not and must not run the organization and especially not micromanage.

I have seen many organizations with great potential not fully leveraging the opportunity and spending more time in leadership politics, which becomes a recipe for disaster. While the board chair and the president are both responsible for any misalignment, I hold the board chair as the main culprit. Here is how I would define the roles in a non-profit organization:

Board of Directors

1. Determine strategic approach
2. Select the most appropriate (selfless) board chair
3. Identify and select the most suitable candidate as organization president
4. Provide support, checks and balances for board chair and president
5. Act as a resourceful Ambassador for the organization
    a. Give time and financial support
    b. Get others involved to support the organization
    c. Assist in opening doors for sponsorship and partnership

Board chair

1. Attract and retain desirable board members while engaging and motivating them to give their best
2. Manage a cordial relationship between the board members and the president
3. Provide oversight and close monitoring on financial growth

4. Provide guidance and coaching to the president

5. Enhance the image and financial health of the organization

President/Executive Director

1. Full operation responsibility including managing staff

2. Overall leadership

3. Fundraising

4. Board development

5. Programs and activities

The board chair should not be the president of the organization as that is a full-time job. The boards without a functional full-time president are highly dependent on luck which should never be a long-term strategy. It is board's responsibility to select a selfless and fearless leader as a board chair. Never appoint anyone a chair who is without prior leadership or C-Suite experience. Some people lobby to become a board chair to satisfy an unfulfilled professional desire. They may have good intentions, but they want to hold the chair position and practice their leadership skills at organization's expense.

The challenges and opportunities at profitable boards are a bit different but the approach along with the roles and responsibilities are quite similar. A board's role is not to provide adult supervision to the organization but to become the extended resource in taking the organization to the next level. Leaders who join boards, especially the non-profit boards primarily to enhance their own image rather than believing in the cause, should not serve the board. It is a mission driven role where the exchange is always giving more than getting.

MANAGING THE BOARD

The board governance for a non-profit or a profitable organization has always been a challenge for many leaders. A good leader always keeps the balance and utilizes the board as a guiding council that provides the support to the executive leader and lets her/him run the organization. Some good leaders have perished fighting the board. This is the most unnecessary problem a leader can be a victim of.

Managing the board is a complex problem. Many leaders inherit boards, and they feel helpless working witha non-supportive board. The bigger the organization, the more challenging the task can be. Here are a few recommendations for leaders to manage the board effectively.

1. Bring the board chair and executive committee into your confidence and gain trust

2. Manage the expectation and communication transparently and regularly. Let them know you need their guidance, not micromanagement

3. Appear fearless but cooperative; make them believe that you can deliver. Remember, they need you more than you need them. Push back when necessary

4. Rotate the board members and bring your own board members. You don't want a rubber stamp board but people who will coach you and support you

5. Deliver results. Under-promise and over-deliver

SUMMARY

- Both managers and leaders are critical in any organization; the skill set for each role is quite different.
- But entrepreneurship pretty much forces you to be a manager and a leader at the same time.
- Although technology facilitates business today significantly, tech devices can distract us from our key responsibilities. Leaders must be aware of when they're distracted and rein in the time we spend on social media, for example.

QUOTES BY TARIQ KHAN

Challenges are the biggest opportunities. Good leaders know that, and great leaders leverage them.

Managers are remembered by their contributions and leaders by their impact.

CHAPTER 6

Diversity, Equity, and Inclusion: Connecting with the Changing Audience—Your Biggest Challenge

CHAPTER LEARNING OBJECTIVES

1. Understand the separate meanings of *diversity*, *equity*, and *inclusion*.
2. Learn why it is a mistake to try to use the same set of knowledge and skills in every future leadership role.
3. Learn a three-phase approach for working with a disengaged and trauma-impacted workforce.
4. Read the insights of three leaders who have demonstrated exemplary leadership in managing diversity, equity, and inclusion while building a thriving workplace.

The concept of diversity, equity, and inclusion (DEI) has become a quintessential topic today, especially in leadership corridors and C-suites. Leaders use it, abuse it, misunderstand it, "check the box" for it, hype it, and underestimate it. Very few leaders have cracked the code on DEI. Let's spend some time exploring the importance of DEI in your leadership journey.

First, let's define these three important concepts:

1. *Diversity* is the differences among us that make us unique. Diversity is a fact; it is what we *are*.
2. *Equity* is a fair opportunity for all, according to each person's need. It requires effort for leaders to create equity in their organization by neutralizing barriers.
3. *Inclusion* is an effort to value others through meaningful engagement. It is a choice.

WHY DOES DIVERSITY MATTER?

Imagine you are working on a project with a team of five, and your job is developing a new product. All team members are same age, gender, racial background, and are almost identical in approach, habits, and thought process.

Now think about another team that is also working on the same project. The second team also has five members, but they all are of different backgrounds, age groups, racial makeup, and multiple gender identities. They are also different in approach, habits, and thought process.

Which team is likely to develop a more innovative product?

Diversity brings a broad perspective and value that a monolithic group most likely does not have. Our customers are not homogeneous; we can serve them better through more diverse representation. Leaders are responsible for ensuring that their organizations reflect the representation of the audiences they serve.

In May 2020, McKinsey & Company released a report titled "How Diversity & Inclusion Matter." The report is based on findings from data collected from fifteen countries and more than one thousand large companies. The report validates diversity as a business case. It also confirms that diversity on executive teams has most likely resulted in increased financial performance over time. The table below clearly demonstrates the outperformance that results from gender diversity and ethnic diversity.[1]

The business case for diversity in executive teams remains strong.

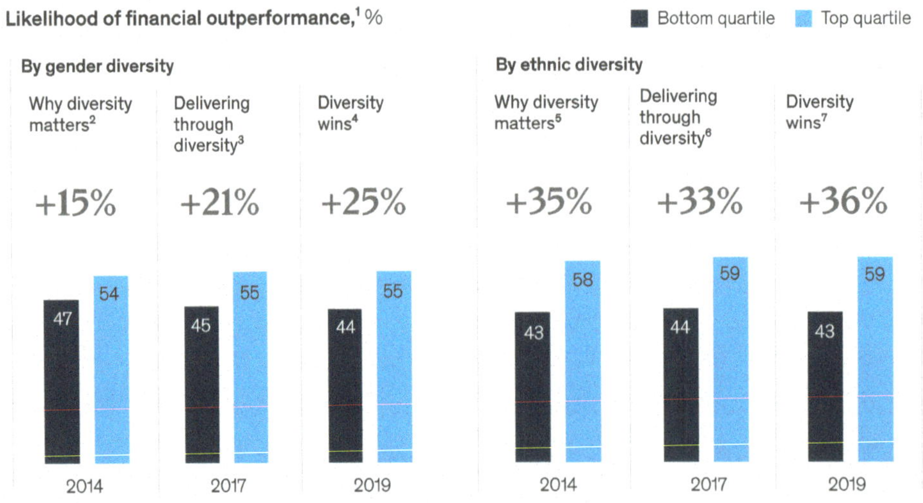

[1]Likelihood of financial outperformance vs the national industry median; p-value <0.05, except 2014 data where p-value <0.1. [2]n = 383; Latin America, UK, and US; earnings before interest and taxes (EBIT) margin 2010–13. [3]n = 991; Australia, Brazil, France, Germany, India, Japan, Mexico, Nigeria, Singapore, South Africa, UK, and US ; EBIT margin 2011–15. [4]n = 1,039; 2017 companies for which gender data available in 2019, plus Denmark, Norway, and Sweden; EBIT margin 2014–18. [5]n = 364; Latin America, UK, and US; EBIT margin 2010–13. [6]n = 589; Brazil, Mexico, Singapore, South Africa, UK, and US; EBIT margin 2011–15. [7]n = 533; Brazil, Mexico, Nigeria, Singapore, South Africa, UK, and US, where ethnicity data available in 2019; EBIT margin 2014–18.
Source: Diversity Wins data set

1. Exhibit from "Diversity wins: How inclusion matters," May 2020, McKinsey & Company, www.mckinsey.com.

I have spent most of my corporate career in the financial services industry. I started my career in sales and got promoted to sales management within two years. The toughest job in that industry is a sales job, yet it is the most rewarding. In a sale-driven organization, salespeople are considered the most valuable employees. The only other job that may be tougher than sales job is of sales management. When I became a sales manager, most of the salespeople in my branch either got transferred or quit. I was among the youngest person in my branch and most senior salespeople were not willing to accept me as their manager.

DIVERSITY AND INCLUSION GO TOGETHER

The time has come when we have to build work environments that are inclusive. The American workforce is becoming more diverse.

Although I feel fortunate to do business and live in a country that embraces *diversity*, our claim to fame for being a "diversity role model" has been challenged in the recent past. We have seen clear polarization, and what has always united us often divides us. I still believe we are one of the most diverse countries in the world, and we will overcome the challenges—eventually. We must remember that *diversity* is incomplete unless *inclusion* is there. Diversity and inclusion (D&I) go together.

Ask yourself, "Am I truly building an organization for the future?"

Even if you are a new leader or entrepreneur, I am sure that you do not want to put an expiration date on your company. I can't think of any leader who would say, "Hey, my company should last till 2030." You want it to be thriving for an eternity; you want it to be indefinite. Leaving a legacy is an unannounced destination for most leaders. The only way to prolong your organization's sustainability is by creating an environment and culture that are adaptive and inclusive. We don't know what that will look like ten years from now. All we know is that it is going to be different from what it is today.

Diversity is not only acknowledging differences; it is also grasping the concept of inclusion. You have to create an environment in which the people who have a more classic outlook on business can at least start to look at things through a different lens. We don't necessarily want them to change completely because their experience and viewpoints are huge assets for us; they enhance our diversity. They simply need to recognize that things are changing.

A fully inclusive perspective considers everyone's point of view. Your responsibility as a leader is to take everyone on your team, whether they are young, old, new, or long-term employees, and bring them into an open network of sharing thoughts and ideas. Your job is not to influence or change people's behavior but to help them adapt at their own pace. This is best accomplished when you can positively influence their attitude. Attitudes lead to behavior.

As a leader, it's important for you to find the alignment between people of diverse thinking, lifestyle, and behavior. We have to think about how we can bring this alignment into a changing environment. If you are only giving orders, you will have a disengaged team. There will eventually be dissent. But if you are adaptable and inclusive, your team will be willing to walk with you on the path to success.

Leaders who are forthcoming, visionary, and able to adapt to changing times and circumstances will be the most successful. The call to action here is for leaders to be more flexible. If your leadership style doesn't allow you to do that, then your sustainability is in question.

Even if you consider yourself a classic leader, you have the power to adapt to different circumstances. In leadership, we must adapt to the challenges we face. It isn't just about asking yourself, "Am I an adaptive leader or not?" but rather, "Am I willing and able to change my way of seeing things?"

EACH LEADERSHIP ROLE REQUIRES A DIFFERENT APPROACH

We learn effective leadership strategies in college, from mentors, and through trial and error. We learn what works with a particular audience and in a particular industry. But we cannot make the mistake of using that set of knowledge and skills in every future leadership role. Each situation requires a unique approach.

Ron Johnson is a perfect example of someone who makes a colossal blunder by viewing all his leadership roles through one lens.

In 2011, Johnson was hired to overhaul the floundering JCPenney retail brand. He had been a star retailer at Apple and Target. He had been responsible for designing Apple stores. If you have ever been to an Apple store, you know it's one of the most phenomenal retail experiences you can have. My kids used to go to Apple just to hang out there. I would ask them, "Why are you going to Apple? Do you need to buy anything?"

They would say, "Well, no. We're just going to go hang out."

The credit for those goes to Ron Johnson and his team.

When he walked into JCPenney, Johnson said, "The store looks very cluttered. This is not how consumers want to be engaged."

Johnson implemented a series of drastic changes at JCPenney to transform the department stores, and he did it without testing them out first, which is standard retail practice. He also made too many changes too quickly at a time when the American economy was not strong. He discontinued the use of sales, coupons, and rebate offers, which customers valued. He discontinued popular private brands like St. John's Bay to make way for more national brands. He revamped the home department to give it an upscale look. But these initiatives backfired because they alienated loyal JCPenney customers instead of attracting them.[2]

Johnson was given unlimited resources to turn the brand around, but he didn't understand the core JCPenney consumer. The people who shopped at Target and Apple were very different from the soccer moms who were perfectly fine with cluttered aisles, as long as they were able to use their coupons and discounts.

---

2. "A Recap of What Went Wrong at JC Penny Under Ron Johnson," Sharon Bailey, *Market Realist*, October 1, 2015, https://marketrealist.com/2015/10/recap-went-wrong-jcpenney-ron-johnson.

The company reported a $985 million annual loss for the year on revenues that had declined twenty-five percent from the previous year to $13 billion, prompting a fifty percent decline in the stock under Johnson's erratic leadership. In TV commercials, JC Penny admitted that the company had "made a mistake" by not listening to its customers.[3]

Johnson did not take the time to understand his new audience. He didn't adjust his knowledge to the new industry, company, and core group of customers. This is a critical lesson to learn: as leaders, we must tailor our approach to every situation.

THE CHANGING FACE OF OUR EMPLOYEES AND CONSUMERS

The United States is the third-largest country in the world in terms of population, followed by China and India. Unlike China and India, though, this is a multicultural country. In China, most of the people are Chinese. Most people in China eat Chinese food, but they don't call it "Chinese food"; they just call it "food." Similarly, most people living in India are of Indian descent.

In the United States, nearly every third person is either Hispanic, Black, or Asian. The ten largest U.S. cities are composed of multicultural majorities. This is a fact that the ten largest U.S. cities have multicultural population as majority.

Although some researchers project that the multicultural population will be a majority in this country around 2044, other experts say this prediction is a misrepresentation of the way people self-identify.

For example, according to a June 2021 article in *The Atlantic*, "The narrative that nonwhite people will soon outnumber white people is not only divisive, but also false." The authors, all professors, say their research on immigration, public opinion, and racial demography reveals that "The majority–minority narrative contributes to our national polarization" by "rigidly splitting Americans into two groups: white versus nonwhite."

Ethnic diversity in the United States makes it a land of opportunity for people from all over the world.

The world around us is changing and changing rapidly. Women have always composed nearly half of world's population, but now, they are playing a much more active role and sitting in the driver's seat in business. We still have a long way to go, though, in creating gender equity. Leaders can make it happen. I hope we will prioritize gender equity to ensure proper representation of women leaders among our ranks.

ADVICE FOR MULTICULTURAL AND WOMEN LEADERS

Thriving in a business environment has always been more difficult for women and people of multicultural ethnicity because they often are not given the same opportunities as men. Some women react to this reality more effectively than others.

3. "JC Penny and the Terrible Cost of Hiring an Outsider CEO," Noel Tichy, *Fortune*, November 13, 2014, http://fortune.com/2014/11/13/jc-penney-ron-johnson-ceo-succession/.

Unfortunately, I have seen many multicultural and women leaders take a defensive approach once they get the top job.

For example, a woman who gets promoted to become the head of an organization becomes extra cautious while building her C-Suite team. If she has to hire ten direct reports and her first five hires are all women, she might not want to hire any more women because she wants to avoid the perception that she is bringing all women into the leadership role. Men typically don't think that way. They will hire all ten men for the leadership roles without a second thought.

I have also seen some multicultural and women leaders who block the entry of more people of color or women into the leadership corridors because they want to stay unique and avoid competition. In my opinion, that is a sign of weakness, not leadership.

Leaders must hire the most talented people and groom them as their replacement. Yes, they must ensure that minorities are properly represented across the board.

But a woman leader doesn't have to act like a man leader to be accepted or considered successful. *She must act like a leader who happens to be a woman.* A woman leader who has not moved the needle on gender diversity during her time in leadership might always be criticized harshly because more was expected of her. Unfairly, we always tend to expect more from women.

NORMALIZING THE POLARIZATION

Leadership is always a challenge and an opportunity. The world witnessed a unique work-related trauma in 2020 and beyond. The COVID-19 pandemic alone has changed the world in many ways.

On a professional level, the biggest asset for any organization is its people (employees, customers, and communities). Organizations worldwide were severely impacted during the pandemic. Simultaneously, we also witnessed external events that brought irreconcilable differences, not only in our leadership positions but also in our behavior.

George Floyd's death in police custody in Minneapolis on May 25, 2020, sparked a new debate of systemic racism and social injustice in the United States and around the world. The support for Black Lives Matter grew significantly and across this country and globally.

The rise in anti-Asian hate crimes in the United States in 2020 and 2021 added fuel to the fire and created a trauma-impacted environment that made many people depressed, anxious, angry, frightened, and feeling helpless. In addition, working from home, along with home schooling children, made workdays even more challenging for parents and caregivers. All this disruption led to an extremely disturbed workforce.

As this environment of exclusion escalates, it begins to normalize the polarity. If not resolved with full commitment and an integrated approach, this can lead to long-term damage.

In my opinion, there is no "one and done" approach to deal with a polarized and distributed workforce. It all begins with humanization and inclusive listening, along with a unifying approach to bring calmness and positivity.

Many companies and leaders reach out to me seeking my advice on achieving DEI in their organizations. I always ask them, "Why do want to do this?"

In most cases, what they don't say is more important than what they say. For example, they might say they want to do the right thing by creating an inclusive environment when really, they are motivated by an improved bottom line or reputation. We must be committed to this effort because it is the right thing to do, or it will be difficult to execute successfully.

MY THREE-PHASE APPROACH TO REACHING OUT TO A DISENGAGED WORKFORCE

In most cases, we do not know what people are really going through. This is even truer if we are connecting with them less frequently and we, or they, are working virtually.

Good leaders will react to the situation promptly. *Great* leaders will take a proactive approach to demonstrate servant leadership. It is absolutely the right thing to do—and also a strong business case.

Here is a summary of my three-phase approach for working with a disengaged and trauma-impacted workforce.

PHASE 1: ASSESSMENT

Leaders need to carefully assess their environments and get a baseline understanding to see challenges and barriers. This is a critical step to diagnose the impact of trauma that exists in the company that might not be visible. Leaders must have substantive, thoughtful discussions with key stakeholders, and engage in active listening, to capture a meaningful temperature. A thorough assessment will help the leaders evaluate and anticipate the best strategic approach.

PHASE 2: STRATEGIC TRANSFORMATION

Strategic transformation starts with open and meaningful communication with an action plan. It is followed by trauma-informed care through radical healing. Proper training is essential to move forward. Leaders must solve the great disconnect by identifying and addressing the gaps that have appeared due to continued crises. A customized approach is required to complement an organization's culture and establish a conducive environment through inclusive engagement. The recommended training will enable leaders to engage their teams through the installation of new goals. The blended training will ensure maximum participation through remote engagement.

PHASE 3: EVALUATION

Evaluation involves reassembling the leaders and team members to evaluate the impact of the training. This effort will help leaders benchmark their progress and validate their strategic transformation.

Time is of the essence for this phase. If left unaddressed, it is likely to create not only loss of revenue but also loss of some great talent. Failure to evaluate can also create a toxic environment of distrust, fear, and anger, along with unexpected and undesirable outcomes.

Today's workforce is more informed and vocal than in the past. People make a conscious decision about whether to join or stay with an organization based partly on their position on social issues. Leaders must take bold steps and state their position. Effective leaders don't follow the popular approach; they follow the right approach. It is critical to remember that you are not only the leader of people who support the majority view but also a leader of the people who support the minority view. A leader must take a position soon and communicate his or her logic for that position.

At times, not taking a position on an important social issue is the real position.

I have witnessed many leaders taking the wrong turn on this and getting lost trying to navigate to an undetermined destination. More often than usual, you don't get a scorecard right away; you have to wait and let history decide your legacy. The legacy you leave is like life insurance—buyers are not there when the benefits are distributed, but the people they leave behind always appreciate those benefits, and the fact that the policy owners make the wise choice to purchase life insurance makes them immortal to the beneficiaries.

EXEMPLARY LEADERS' THOUGHTS ON DIVERSITY, EQUITY, AND INCLUSION

I reached out to some leaders who have demonstrated exemplary leadership in managing DEI while building a thriving workplace. Here is the wisdom they shared.

1. MARION BROOKS, MBA, VICE PRESIDENT AND U.S. COUNTRY HEAD, DIVERSITY & INCLUSION, NOVARTIS

Marion Brooks is a visionary leader who has an uncompromised passion for promoting diversity and making inclusion a requirement. I asked him for his advice to leaders on DEI, and here is what he shared:

> Diversity, equity, and inclusion are no longer a nice to have, or only the right thing to do. DEI has become a competitive advantage or disadvantage. If you look at all the research, diverse organizations and teams offer three distinct advantages over more homogeneous teams and organizations. They deliver higher revenues, they are more innovative, and they're more responsive to customer needs.

It doesn't matter if it's a Little League team or a major corporation, you want to deliver on those three critical components of success. To accomplish that goal, all three elements of DEI are required. As the old saying goes, diversity is being invited to the dance, inclusion is being asked to dance, and equity is being given an opportunity to select the next song.

Here are a few recommendations on how to embed DEI into the DNA of your organization:

1. Start with the numbers—Look at the demographic makeup of your organization, especially your leadership team, and compare your gender and ethnic diversity numbers to the available talent for similar roles based on the U.S. Census data. This will give you a clear view of where you are doing well and where there are areas of opportunities.

There is no room for excuses here; there are qualified diverse candidates for every role, regardless of industry. The question you have to ask is, "Where we are recruiting, and do we have the reputation of inclusion and advancement of diversity to attract the top talent?"

2. Remove unconscious bias; establish hiring guidelines—Research shows if you have only one woman or person of color in a candidate pool, statistically, they have no chance of receiving an offer. By adding one more qualified woman or person of color, the percentage jumps to over fifty percent that one of the diverse candidates could receive an offer. The inclusion of another qualified candidate disrupts the unconscious confirmation bias.

3. Establish or leverage employee resource groups—This can help you formulate and execute your DEI strategy.

2. ANNA MOK, COFOUNDER, PRESIDENT, AND CHAIRWOMAN OF THE BOARD, ASCEND LEADERSHIP

I have known Anna Mok for many years and have served on a few nonprofits with her. Anna is an extremely successful professional with a global organization. She is an amazing mother, friend, professional, and most importantly a woman with the highest commitment to social causes. Over the years, I have seen her give a lot more than she has gotten back.

Here are Anna's thoughts on how leaders can bring their passion to social causes:

> I consider myself an accidental activist. My passion for social causes, especially in ensuring economic and educational access for all, stemmed from my own experiences as an Asian American woman in the corporate world, raised by immigrant parents. I realized, while studying at the University of California, Berkeley, that many people, including immigrants and children of immigrants, face societal and cultural barriers that impede their ability to reach their potential in many aspects of American life.

I saw relatively early in my career that Asian Americans, women, and diverse communities were being represented in growing numbers in the workplace, but they were not advancing to positions of leadership at the same pace as their largely male and white colleagues. That led me to cofound Ascend, the largest nonprofit Pan-Asian organization for business professionals in North America. We focus on helping our members reach their full potential and, in turn, drive greater workplace and societal impact. For me, helping create greater access and advancement for *all* is one of the most important ways I felt I could help affect change as a corporate leader.

I understand that what happens in our personal lives impacts how we show up and lead in our workplaces. As a leader, you should strive to have the best people on your team and at the table with you. If long-term systemic inequities are preventing qualified people from gaining access to opportunities and keeping them from bringing their contributions to your talent pool, then one of the most important and impactful things you can do is address and remove the impediments to access.

At the end of the day, for a leader, it's about people—it's about caring about people, our fellow human beings. It's about recognizing not just each person's unique "superpower," but the totality of their existence and experiences, and not just how they present at work, and then bringing out their full potential. We need to create the conditions for all people to have equal access and the opportunities to be their full selves without some of the limiting societal constrictions and restrictions that are unfortunately still in place.

Companies and corporations are not normally associated with social justice work, but 2020 shifted the paradigm. Companies and leaders who want to be sustainable and successful cannot sidestep hard discussions. They have both a moral and fiduciary obligation to understand the issues, create inclusive workplaces, support their employees and communities, and do what is in their individual and collective power to advance social justice and positive change.

While the pandemic has challenged almost all organizations, educational institutions faced the most unique challenge that many were not prepared for a situation of this magnitude. Many academic institutions had several dissatisfied students, faculty members, and staff. One institution that stood out while leading through the pandemic, effectively managing diversity and accommodating international students, is my own—New York University (NYU). NYU is among the largest private university in the world and has the largest representation of international students in the world.

The credit for this exemplary leadership goes to the entire team at NYU, especially to NYU President Andrew Hamilton and NYU SVP, Global Inclusion and Strategic Innovation, Dr. Lisa Coleman. It was an arduous job to manage and lead the most diverse university with more than fifty thousand students, faculty members, and staff. I was most impressed with the timely, bold, and transparent communication NYU's leaders sent out throughout the pandemic.

3. DR. LISA COLEMAN, PHD, SVP, GLOBAL INCLUSION AND STRATEGIC INNOVATION, NEW YORK UNIVERSITY

I have known Dr. Lisa Coleman for a few years and got to know her well during the pandemic. I truly admire her contributions to the university and the entire diverse community. I asked Lisa to share her thoughts about the changing environment and leading through DEI. Here is what she told me:

> When I think about individuals from underrepresented communities and backgrounds across organizers, I do not think of problems, risks, or patronage; I see solutions, assets, possibilities, and innovation. Far too often, leaders respond to diversity, inclusion, equity, and access (DEIA) with a deficit-based, patronage, reactive, and/or crisis, risk-mitigation approach. This approach does not position leaders or organizations to advance DEIA through a strength-based model in their organizations, which we know from the research is a prerequisite for innovation and is also crucial for acceleration and working with emerging generations, as well as ensuring future-readiness.
>
> Furthermore, crisis/deficit models often position organizations for failure because they lack the ability to instill systematic structures and systems that are strategic in leveraging opportunities. To be prepared for future pandemics, market downturns, etc., there is a need for increased accountability and to ensure the infrastructures of DEIA are in place to guard against, as well as move the needle on, current disparities. This type of positioning organizations to accelerate DEIA, even during times of crisis.
>
> As much research demonstrates, leaders focused on inclusivity will need to proactively lead with DEIA in everything they do, including ensuring appropriate resource allocation aligned to a robust organizational strategy and assessment process for DEI. Resources will include time, money, people, research, focus, etc. similar to any other area such as marketing or IT.
>
> Through this praxis, organizations are better positioned to cultivate more inclusive and equitable organizational cultures, teaming structures, strategies, and business plans/models where diversity is leveraged as one of the key drivers for success and enhanced innovation. Again, leaders must approach DEIA with the same discipline as they would R&D, marketing, strategic planning, IT, etc. listening to their teams and colleagues with expertise and holding themselves and their organizations accountable to progress and outcomes. Leaders must also be attentive to succession planning to ensure sustainability; this is directly related to global shifts in demography, diversification of emerging generations, and the future of innovation.
>
> It is not always easy, but research demonstrates that contestation within organizations, including around DEIA, might be leaned into, listened to, and leveraged, rather than snuffed out, avoided, and eliminated. This type of engagement might lead to all types of new and different ideas and emerging practices.

Bottom line, what we know from research on transgenerational diversity and working with the emerging generations of leaders, is that if current leaders do not implement a DEIA-centered approach, they will not be able to harness the innovation, or the talent needed for the future. The question for me is always "How not to be Blockbuster, Altavista, or Netscape?" And this will mean organizations will need to pivot and ready themselves for the incredibly globally diverse future that has already begun to emerge.

Today, it is practically impossible for any leader to accomplish greatness without fully embracing diversity, ensuring equity, and practicing inclusion. Every leader must create a scorecard on DEI and self-evaluate himself or herself.

Great leaders can't lie to themselves. People around you are changing rapidly, and the old bravado might not work on them for long. Connecting favorably with your new and existing talent will give you a longer lease for your leadership, history may remember you more kindly.

SUMMARY

- Diversity brings a broad perspective and value that a monolithic group most likely does not have. Our customers are not homogeneous; we can serve them better through more diverse representation.
- The only way to prolong your organization's sustainability is by creating an environment and culture that are adaptive and inclusive. We don't know what that will look like ten years from now. All we know is that it is going to be different from what it is today.
- A woman leader doesn't have to act like a male leader to be accepted or considered successful. She must act like a leader who happens to be a woman.
- Many times, people have unconscious bias. Leaders must be aware of this type of insidious threat to a cohesive workforce and eradicate it.

QUOTES BY TARIQ KHAN

Leaders are mortal, leadership can be immortal.

All leaders are not equal.

CHAPTER 7

Classic Leadership versus Adaptive Leadership

CHAPTER LEARNING OBJECTIVES

1. Examine four types of classic (old-style) leadership that lack the key element of adaptability.
2. Understand three reasons why we need more adaptive leaders who continually adapt to their circumstances.
3. Learn how a more diverse population is impacting the way leaders hire talent.

Classic styles of leadership lack the element of adaptability, which is essential for successful leadership today. The best idea in the company might come from a new intern. We need to think of every team member, at every level of the hierarchy, as an asset.

The generation that is coming into the workforce today will find a work environment suffocating if they are not heard or if their creativity is restricted.

CLASSIC LEADERSHIP = THE OLD STYLE

Classic leadership is old! It's outdated. It's the umbrella term that encompasses four of traditional leadership styles:

1. Autocratic
2. Democratic
3. Laissez-faire
4. Bureaucratic

Let's look at each of these classic leadership styles and evaluate what works, what doesn't work, and what is less than ideal about each one.

1. AUTOCRATIC LEADERSHIP

Autocratic leadership can also be called *leadership by fear*. This is a leader-based approach. All the decision-making power is in the hands of the leader. There is no consultation or input from team members.

It is a somewhat military-style leadership approach, and any punishments or rewards are based on the leader's will. There is often a low level of trust between team members and leadership. This leadership style has been criticized throughout the years, especially by the younger generations entering the workforce, who find it difficult to work for an autocratic leader.

Autocratic leaders are this way by nature, and they are used to making decisions on their own, without input from others. A leader might not seek out the opinions of his or her team for several reasons:

1. The team is composed of people who are new to the organization and haven't proved their worth or contribution.
2. The team is untrained and needs more coaching before they can be trusted.
3. The decision needs to be made quickly, and there is no time to consult with others.
4. The leader is confident in his or her own ability to make decisions.

In the first three cases, the leader might be right about not including staff members in important decision making. However, if the leader does not seek the opinions of others simply because he or she is confident, this can cause some pushback from employees.

Autocratic leadership tends to work best if there is a team that is very diverse or undecided on certain subjects. In this case, there might not be as much pushback. However, this style can lead to unhappy team members. They can become resentful and feel excluded, causing low collective morale. It also leads to lower retention rates because talented people will leave the organization if they are not involved in decision making.

2. DEMOCRATIC LEADERSHIP

I like to describe democratic leadership as *leadership by love*. This style is inclusive and is characterized by shared responsibilities and an engaging culture. The leader acts as a coach and trusts his or her team. Recognition is a common practice, and high achievers are generously rewarded.

Democratic leaders always keep their teams informed of what's going on. They play the role of an advisor and have a lot of trust in their team. Delegating tasks is common because the leader is confident that the task will be executed effectively. A democratic leadership style often leads to a happy work environment in which the staff can develop their own goals, and their opinions are valued. Because everyone has more skin in the game and direct ownership of projects, there are higher levels of productivity. Recognition is commonplace, and team members can be developed into genuine leaders.

3. LAISSEZ-FAIRE LEADERSHIP

The next type of classic leadership, laissez-faire leadership, can also be called *leadership by delegation.* This is a leadership style based on a hands-off culture in which the leader delegates the workload to members of the team. The leader is often less engaged and has a team of highly skilled people running the day-to-day operations of the business. The staff is left to manage themselves, and the leader does not feel the need to be involved in all the decision making.

A laissez-faire leader does not provide a lot of guidance or direction and has confidence that the business will run on its own. Team members under this style of leadership are empowered and have authority; however, with lack of direction, they might sometimes feel insecure and desire more supervision. One major downfall of this type of hands-off leadership is that problems can evolve that could have been avoided if there had been more direct involvement from the leader. Also, if the leader is a visionary, his or her vision might not be executed in the ideal way because he or she is not there to supervise. This leadership style is hit or miss in terms of its level of success.

This leadership style can be effective if you have highly skilled team members whom you completely trust, and you know they will deliver on whatever's needed. When your employees feel like they are leaders themselves, you are essentially an outside coach, and you have little involvement in decisions. You might get a lot of surprises in this type of environment, and the surprise might include losing your business completely because you have outsourced your leadership responsibilities to your staff.

Also, if you are a visionary leader, you might not have a team that is as visionary as you are, so your vision might not get executed the way you intended.

4. BUREAUCRATIC LEADERSHIP

A bureaucratic leader practices *leadership by regulation.* The leader is instructional, offers regimented supervision, and expects structured implementation of established rules. This is a predictable style of leadership that is run by the book. The guidelines must be followed, and there is little room for creativity.

There are certain types of work for which this type of leadership is quite effective. For example, in air traffic control or a regulatory industry, there are strict guidelines that must be followed to ensure safety and security. The leader is the regulator who enforces the policies, and no deviation or innovation is required or encouraged. This type of leadership makes it difficult to manage innovative and creative people.

WHAT WE NEED TODAY: ADAPTIVE LEADERSHIP

Now I want to move on to the most relevant leadership style today: *adaptive leadership*. Although this is not a new concept, it is gaining more ground now because virtually every leader has to be adaptive to succeed in today's ever-changing business climate. Adaptive leadership is where a leader can become a visionary—not only thinking of today but also envisioning how the business can be positioned for success five, ten, or twenty years from now.

Take, for example, a new company that is small and local. In the past, it was practically impossible for a smaller new business to compete with major companies. Today, however, with the internet and social media, a new company can compete with any company across the globe. For instance, someone could create a beverage formula in their kitchen or garage, patent their product, go on social media, and compete with companies like Coke and Pepsi. This was never possible before.

This is what Airbnb accomplished. If anybody had said twenty years ago, "I want to compete with Marriott or Hilton," they would have sounded crazy. To accomplish this, a new company would have to build properties worldwide. But in today's flexible, adaptable business climate, Airbnb was able to enter the hospitality scene without owning any real estate and become one of the largest lodging companies in the world. This is a result of adaptive leadership.

This is a more fluid style of leadership. Leaders must continually adapt to their circumstances. There are three main reasons we need more adaptive leaders today:

1. Employees and their expectations about the work environment are changing.
2. Products and services are changing.
3. Territories are changing.

Now let's look at how each one of these factors has impacted the need for adaptive leaders.

1. EMPLOYEES ARE CHANGING

Many major companies today, including Google, Apple, and IBM, no longer require that new hires have college degrees. In the past, the thought of someone without a college degree being hired for certain positions was unheard of.

Are we finally hiring people on merit? It seems so. After all, what does a college degree really mean? If you had a 4.0 GPA in college, all that tells me is that you can memorize things well and retain information in your short-term memory. It doesn't tell me your skill level, the extent of your creativity, or your work style. All it demonstrates is how many hours have been completed in a classroom—but how does this translate to business acumen? We are now hiring a workforce that is going to teach us what we didn't learn in college.

In the past, there was a strict set of guidelines used when a company hired new employees. The checklist to even get in the door for an interview included having a college degree and having a set amount of relevant experience. That is how potential employees were judged, but when they got to work, how relevant were these standards? In some industries, a degree is required. For instance, if you are becoming an actuary, you will probably need a degree in actuarial studies. However, if you are going into a field that fosters creativity and competitive strategy, the fact that you have a degree only tells me that you have been studious in your life, not how well you will perform as an employee in the real world. I have seen that many college dropouts have become phenomenally successful in their careers.

Hiring people who are adaptive means that we are hiring people who will bring a diverse perspective to a group. Maybe they don't understand the language we speak or the culture we live in. We are hiring people with a completely different perspective than we are used to, and that is an asset. But this diversity requires leaders to be adaptive. Today, leaders need to adapt themselves to their employees instead of expecting their employees to adapt themselves to the company. That's an expectation of the past.

Our employees are changing. We are hiring employees more on their skill and merit and less on what it says on their résumés. Employees will come from different parts of the world. We might not be able to see them face-to-face every day because they will be working remotely.

Eventually, we will be hiring machines to do our jobs. We have not been trained to interview robots, but that is going to happen. All these factors make it essential for today's leaders to be adaptive to the changing times we are living in.

2. PRODUCTS AND SERVICES ARE CHANGING

You might wonder why we need adaptive leaders if our products and services are changing. One good reason is the fact that many of today's products might be gone in the next ten years.

I used to use a payphone, a watch, a flashlight, a tape recorder, a boombox, a desktop home computer, an action camera, a calculator, an alarm clock, a notebook, a credit card, a compass, and a navigation system. I could go on and on. These are distinctly individual items made by different companies. Yes, you can still go into the store and buy a calculator, or a watch, or an alarm clock. But one product has come along that has replaced all these products: the smartphone. This one product is taking over the functions of many different companies that were all very good at their craft. The company that was making calculators, and was making them well, might be out of business soon. Think about the kids who are being born today. Will they ever buy a calculator as a separate product? No, they will not.

There are two important accessories that we never leave home without: our phones and our wallets. Only one will survive the times. Guess which one? If you were a manufacturer of wallets, how would you feel about survival? Kodak never imagined in 1980 or 1990 that they would eventually have fewer than 5,000 employees when they used to have 120,000 employees. People have taken picture for a long time, but now, most people take pictures using their phones, not cameras with films.

Let's look at another example: Sony. It was one of the leading television manufacturers in the world. Samsung then came into the market and competed for the top spot. Sony intentionally gave in and said, "OK, you can be the number one market share holder for televisions." Why? Because Sony realized that television manufacturing would be a thing of the past. The adaptive leadership at Sony was able to navigate the changing times and keep the company on track with what will be happening in the future. Today Sony makes PlayStation and video games.

Think about other products we use every day, like pens. We all use pens. Now, think of children who are being born today. How often do you think they will use a pen? Probably not very often. They will type. I remember that people used to go to typing school. Today's generation, the millennials, do not need typing school. They can learn how to use a keyboard faster than any of us, without going to school. If you think back, when hiring, we used to ask candidates their typing speed. If you ask millennials that question, they will say, "What?" They have no idea why they would be asked that question.

A classic, old-school leader who is not adaptive faces a huge challenge, especially with the younger generations entering the workforce.

My daughter has now graduated from college. When she got her first cell phone, she was very excited about it. At that time, we used to wait until kids were twelve or thirteen to give them phones. Now, kids seem to be born with a phone in their hands. A year after she got her first phone, she came to me and asked, "Dad, can you buy me a phone that doesn't make phone calls?"

I asked, "What do you mean?"

As an older person, I was having a difficult time understanding what she was asking. She then explained to me that she didn't use her phone to call people, but only to text. She asked me to look at my phone bill. Sure enough, she was sending about 8,000 texts and making 24 phone calls a month. I was making 5,000 calls and sending only 50 texts. When I thought about it, I realized we might eventually have phones that do not make phone calls.

Younger people rarely call those they know; they text instead. Today, people communicate differently. An adaptive leader will have the capacity to think outside the box, whereas a classic leader might not even recognize that the needs for their products and services are changing.

I challenge you, as a leader, to think about the product or service your company is offering today. Ask yourself, with full honesty and independent thinking, what the future looks like for that product or service five to ten years from now. It is your job as a leader to identify these changes and to transition your company into offering a more relevant product or service that will survive the times.

3. TERRITORIES ARE CHANGING

In the past, leaders had territories. They would say, "I do my business in New York," or "I do my business in the southeastern United States." Today, there is no such thing as local or domestic clients.

Customers can come from anywhere because the internet has no boundaries. As a leader, even if your business is in a specific location, you cannot *just* be a local leader. Your business might be local, but your customers are global. You need to adopt a global leadership style.

What do I mean by *global leadership style*? In my entire career, my best learning has come through traveling to different parts of the world. You might think your product or service is working fine, but then you go and immerse yourself in another culture, and you see things differently. You have to understand that as a leader, you will be managing people who are coming from different cultures and different backgrounds. Valuing and adapting to what people in a different part of the world see can help you imagine the direction your product or service needs to go to stay relevant.

I traveled to a conference in Pakistan a few months ago. There were nine speakers, six who flew from the United States. Many of them were visiting Pakistan for the first time, and they were very overwhelmed and stunned. Although Pakistan is the fifth largest country in the world, its population is one of the youngest, with seventy percent being under the age of forty. We were in a car, and I asked one of the American speakers what he was thinking.

He said, "You know, I see two classes: very rich people and very poor people, but everyone has a cell phone."

I said, "Yeah, but do you know how much a cell phone costs in Pakistan?"

He said, "No. Doesn't it cost the same as it costs in the United States?"

Then in front of him, I asked the driver how much he paid for his phone. He said $16.

A $16 phone might not have much value in the United States, but because Pakistan is young and adaptive, it is one of the fastest growing markets for cell phones. Companies realized that this is a growing trend but that not everyone can afford a $300 or $1,000 phone. As a result, they began creating affordable phones. So, while there might not be a market for your product or service in one part of the world, there might be in another part. But you can capitalize on the opportunity only if you are adaptive.

Have you thought about taking your business global? Today, taking a business to a global level does not require the same commitment as it did in the 1990s or even the early 2000s. It can open many new markets for your business. As a global adaptive leader, you must ask yourself how you can expand your business globally. If you find a local market saturated, but you are open to new ideas and adaptation, consider selling in entirely different territories. The opportunities for your business will be endless.

Of course, there are many complications associated with entering a new market, and it might not be as simple. Leaders leading large organizations might not be able to grow globally if this is not a part of their strategy. Imagine finding out that your biggest competitor is now going global. Would you revisit your strategy?

ADAPTING TO DIVERSE THINKING, LIFESTYLE, AND BEHAVIORS ISN'T OPTIONAL

Adapting is no longer optional. While we are predicting products or services and their places in the long-term picture of our organizations and society, we also much adjust our mindset. Many of us, including me, are a part of Gen X. I came from traditional schooling, and I had a somewhat difficult time learning to become an adaptive leader.

Leaders who have been schooled in more recent times tend to have more of an adaptive nature. They are changing with the times. A smart business leader, in the short term, will adapt immediately to changing demands. Adapting doesn't mean giving up; it means you're changing yourself. A few years ago, we were at an office retreat, discussing how to become more productive. One of our young and new team members suggested that we should make it a four-day work week and take off Fridays. All were stunned, especially the older people. Nevertheless, we all liked the idea. I said, let's do it and everyone will be available, if needed. Since then, we never had an urge to go back to five-day work week.

A few years ago, I insisted that I would reply to text messages in full sentences. I felt like it was poor English to write with emojis. However, when I tried to force this on my kids, they said, "No way!" Guess what? I had to adapt to the new way of texting. Today, no one complains that you did not write "thank you" out completely. In fact, a thumbs-up emoji is perfectly acceptable. Don't view it as giving up; instead, realize that you are adapting to what is right in front of you.

SUMMARY

- Classic styles of leadership lack the element of adaptability, which is essential for successful leadership today.
- A smart business leader, in the short term, will adapt immediately to changing demands. Adapting doesn't mean giving up; it means you're changing yourself.
- There are two important accessories that we never leave home without: our phones and our wallets. Only one will survive the times.
- The generation that is coming into the workforce today will find a work environment suffocating if they are not heard or if their creativity is restricted.

QUOTES BY TARIQ KHAN

Like leader, like follower.

Leader in a tough time is an orphan.

CHAPTER 8

The Future of Education

CHAPTER LEARNING OBJECTIVES

1. Learn how our traditional education system is not aligned with the way babies and children develop skills naturally, along with six ways we can improve learning.
2. Understand the difference between synchronous learning and asynchronous learning.
3. Explore how AI will transform education in the future.
4. Read the success story of innovator and WhatsApp founder Jan Koum.

When we are born, and as we go through childhood, we are learning machines. Thanks to the human nervous system, we can learn how to speak a language without any textbooks, lectures, or tests. This is the style of learning we are born with. We figure it out by having our parents talk to us and teach us—immersion. By the time we enter kindergarten, we know how to speak our native language.

Anything a child learns early in life is done without textbooks or regimented training. This includes potty training, walking, and climbing on a chair to get into the cookie jar. But then, the moment children enter school, they are exposed to a structured learning style, all the way through elementary school, middle school, high school, and college. Plus, the focus is on their grade point average, not on learning. To succeed, students need to get high scores on standardized tests.

Recently, I sat down with some of the people I attended middle school with more than thirty years ago. We talked about everybody in our class and where they are today. The people in our middle school who had top grades are doing okay, but those who had failing grades are doing extremely well. The rebellious backbenchers have turned out to be street-smart and successful. However, I don't want to underestimate the academically smart people. They are gifted and hardworking. Many of them are gift to this world and have made great innovations.

The subjects I learned in school, like algebra and chemistry, are not the skills I am using today. I was basically a copy-and-paste machine in school. I forcefully memorized everything for my exams and then forgot it shortly afterward. I was taught to ask the question, "Is this going to be on the test?" If the answer was no, then I didn't bother learning it. After my school years, I learned "soft" skills, such as communication and negotiation, which are the skills that have led me to be successful.

We need to challenge the education system. It is not child-led. Instead, it is led by a structured learning model that was created hundreds of years ago. We think it's working, but it's not. If you look at today's high school and college students, the most successful ones are usually learning ***outside*** the classroom.

WE MUST LET CHILDREN DISCOVER THEIR PERSONALITIES AND INTERESTS

When I began my undergraduate studies, I was a computer science major. That was in the mid- to late 1980s, when the field of computer information systems was a happening thing, and I was very excited. But when I took my first computer class, I hated it. I struggled throughout the class. Toward the end of the class, I struggled really hard to pass the class because I couldn't afford to retake the class.

When the class ended, I went to my academic advisor and told her, "I think I misjudged my major. I'm not interested in computer information systems."

She said, "Tell me more about it."

I said, "I like coming to college. I like making friends. I enjoy being in the class. I just don't like exams, and I hate reading boring textbooks."

She asked me, "What do you want to do?"

I replied, "I would like to get into a career where I can travel the world, meet lots of people, make lots of money, and don't have to come to the office every day."

She looked at me, laughed, and said, "Try marketing."

So, I took a class in marketing, and I fell in love with it. What I learned from that experience is that sometimes we mismatch ourselves to our opportunities. There could be several reasons for this. Maybe the market or economy is very good for a certain field at a certain point in time. Sometimes it's because as Asian Americans, our parents force us to get into the majors that are more popular. Asian American parents often want their kids to be doctors, lawyers, or engineers and graduate from top schools.

Whatever the reason, many of us don't follow our passion. We don't really understand what we want to do or what we would excel at. My personal experience gave me a good understanding of how many people are mismatched to their life's work, sometimes because someone else has forced them into majors they don't enjoy. And then, when they graduate, their learning experience is limited to some textbooks, which they completely get rid of right after they graduate.

Too often, academic learning is limited to memorizing facts from boring textbooks for a short period of time. Most of us never go back to those textbooks, and we seldom retain that knowledge. Of course, the overall higher education experience is quite rewarding, but it has not changed much in many decades.

TEST-OPTIONAL UNIVERSITIES ARE ON THE RISE

In a growing trend, universities are no longer requiring the SAT and ACT tests for college admission. In fact, as of May 2020, there were more than 1,000 universities across the United States that no longer require those standardized tests for admission. They are relying on other criteria to determine if a student should be admitted.[1]

I think this is a positive development. Years ago, when I took the GMAT to get into business school, I studied hard and passed it, but did I learn anything? No. I have no idea what types of questions were on the test. There may have been a logical reason for administering these tests eighty years ago, but I don't know if that logic is relevant today.

We have seen some great disruptors in the past few decades, but I'm not sure if we can give all the credit to the education system. I don't believe monitored exams tell us much about students. All they tell us is that one is better than another at memorizing facts from a textbook, which they can keep in their minds for a short period of time. But that is no reflection on how well they are going to do in life.

LIFE IS MUCH DIFFERENT FROM THE ACADEMIC LEARNING ENVIRONMENT

People end up learning some of life's biggest lessons through trial and error because many valuable life skills aren't taught in the classroom.

Why don't we teach students about corporate politics, or shall we call it corporate arts, which is one of the most important topics in corporate America? Why don't we teach them how to succeed as entrepreneurs and how to recover from mistakes and failures in those endeavors? Why don't we teach them how to obtain venture capital funding for a start-up and also about business development, which entrepreneurs spend a lot of time and effort on? Another practical skill that business owners use daily is prospecting, but people typically don't learn how to do that until they have graduated. We should teach all these important skills *during* the educational process, not after.

Some students are fortunate enough to have parents who spend time teaching and challenging them. But many do not. This is why I believe many kids who come from dysfunctional homes end up succeeding in life—they are forced, from a young age, to survive on the streets. They learn how to stand up for themselves, how to survive. That teaches them a lot more about life than sitting in nice homes, screen timing and playing video games.

1. "Test-Optional Colleges: List of Colleges NOT Requiring SAT Scores," Marissa Daniel, College Life Today, May 28, 2020, https://www.collegelifetoday.com/tips/organizing/college-not-requiring-sat/.

A lot of parents, me included, find it upsetting when our children spend so much time staring at the screens on their phones and other devices. Now, I'm not against these devices because they are the future. Can we really tell them to limit their screen time or stay off those devices that provide them access to the world? No, but there is a difference between using a device as a learning tool and being addicted to some of the apps on it.

The study-abroad programs that many universities offer students is a great concept for teaching real-life skills. Students visit another country for one or two weeks as part of some MBA programs. But what can you learn in a couple of weeks about a different country or a culture? Some study-abroad programs last for an entire semester, and I believe that provides more of an immersive and useful experience. I envision some type of extension of that program that enables students to really learn about different cultures and people.

I believe it should be mandatory, a graduation requirement, for students to get practical training by working outside their college curricula during a degree program. If students had to work during their studies, maybe for six months, I believe it would complement their classroom studies in an incredibly beneficial way. They could come back to the classroom and discuss with the instructor and other students what they've learned in the real world.

I try to bring real-life experience into my pedagogy. All my students have to work in a group and develop a marketing plan or turnaround leadership strategy for a failing company. This is their assignment for the semester. They learn subject matter expertise in each class and then apply that into their group project, which they present as team on the last day of the semester.

A few years ago, I assigned one of my competitive strategy classes to develop a competitive strategy for a leading retail company. I happen to know a senior marketing executive in that company and asked her if she would like to come to my final class to see the presentations about her company. My friend got really excited about it and flew in from out of state to attend my final class. A total of five groups presented their strategies, and my friend saw all these presentations.

After the class, I took her out for coffee and asked her for feedback. I noticed that she was quiet after the class and seemed preoccupied. I asked her if everything was all right. She replied "Yeah" unconvincingly. First, I thought she didn't like my class, and it may have been a waste of her time (three hours). I insisted then that she finally open up.

Her reply was, "Tariq, after seeing these class presentations, I feel like going back to my office and firing my marketing team. The ideas your students have presented amazed me. How can they come up with ideas without all the resources my team has?"

She was angry, but I was not!

SYNCHRONOUS VERSUS ASYNCHRONOUS LEARNING

The COVID-19 pandemic has challenged the education system to be more virtual and blended, in many cases. Virtual online teaching was a reaction to the need to continue education remotely. However, COVID-19 brought us closer to what was imminent: distance learning. Virtual learning became a common practice. Once the mature generation cracked the code and learned to hold meetings via virtual platforms, it became a far more acceptable mode of communication.

Most learning institutions adapted quickly to shift to a fully virtual or blended teaching model. However, the students, teachers, and parents—in that order—who were responsible for homeschooling suffered the most in 2020 and 2021. It became a moment of truth for the learning fraternity.

Research has been done on the benefits of both synchronous and asynchronous learning.

Synchronous learning refers to all types of learning in which both instructors and students are in the same place, at the same time. This includes in-person classes and live online meetings when the whole class or smaller groups meet on a virtual communication platform. With synchronous learning, students usually proceed down the learning path together, with the instructor providing them with guidance as they complete activities.

Asynchronous learning is a student-centered teaching method that is used often in online learning. The basic premise is that learning can occur at different times in different locations for each student. With asynchronous learning, instructors usually create a learning path that students follow at their own pace.

Most online teaching happens asynchronously. Synchronous learning usually takes place only if there is a specific need for live discussion or interaction.

Some experts in the educational community worry that remote instruction could further widen equity gaps among students. Previous research shows that students who take courses online are less likely to persist than their peers who take courses face-to-face. Also, underrepresented minority students often have lower performance than other groups in online courses.[2]

But some say it's not online learning itself or asynchronous learning that leads to disparities; rather, what matters is how a course is designed.

According to Jessica Rowland Williams, director of Every Learner Everywhere, a network of organizations aiming to improve teaching and learning with technology, simply moving a lecture-based class to an online format is not going to work for more vulnerable students. The focus, she says, should be on distributing the benefits of learning across a broad range of learners. She recommends setting up peer-support groups so students can help each other build skills while also building a sense of community along the way. She also suggests that faculty give students options. For example, instructors could provide a recorded version of synchronous class events. That way, students who need to work or care for children or family and cannot participate in the live sessions won't fall behind because of scheduling conflicts.[3]

Some faculty members use tools like Google Docs and Hypothesis to let students annotate documents or websites. Their classmates can then respond to their annotations and build conversations.

2. "The Moment Is Primed for Asynchronous Learning," Madeline St. Amour, Inside Higher Ed, September 16, 2020, https://www.insidehighered.com/news/2020/09/16/dont-dismiss-asynchronous-learning-experts-say-improve-it.
3. Ibid.

I mostly teach face-to-face classes in the Fall and Spring semester. Few years ago, I started teaching asynchronous classes. Initially, I was a bit uncomfortable with the self-paced format, but it really worked out well. Now I teach that every summer and it allows me to be anywhere in the world, just like my students, and teach the course while learning. The 2020 and 2021 blended version was quite challenging, but we survived. Humans are the most flexible when they need to be.

OUR SKILLS CHANGE OVER TIME

Decades ago, people wrote everything down with pens and pencils. Then typewriters came along, and then computers. In another forty years, they may forget how to write!

I used to be able to write in several languages. I can still speak them, but I don't write them well anymore because I don't write much in those languages. Babies who are born today will most likely have very little exposure to writing; they will type on computers, for the most part. As time goes on, we get weaker in some skills and stronger in others. When self-driving cars become the norm, many people will no longer drive, and young people will never have a reason to learn how to drive.

The world is changing in many ways, but education has not changed much at all.

When Jeff Bezos launched Amazon.com in 1994, he wanted to sell books initially. He did that very successfully, and then he started selling music. Then he wrote a letter to all his top clients and asked them, "What else do you want us to sell?" The responses he got were unexpected. One client said he really needed windshield wipers. Other clients mentioned similarly random items. Bezos realized he could sell anything.

Amazon's success can largely be attributed to its flexibility. By asking what people wanted and accommodating those requests, Amazon became the most flexible company in the world. They had warehouses built with advanced automation to make distribution of every imaginable item possible quickly. Education needs to be just as flexible.

SIX WAYS WE CAN IMPROVE LEARNING

So how do we fix education so that it allows students to enjoy exploring who they are becoming? I don't have a magic wand, but I do have some ideas that I think we need to consider.

1. START OUT WITH CHILD-LED LEARNING

First of all, when young children go to kindergarten or pre-kindergarten, I believe that first experience with education should be child-led, like a Montessori school. Many European countries do that. In a child-led program, children get to explore their creativity and let their personalities unfold.

In the U.S. education system, which is a kindergarten system, five-year-olds have a lot of books, including math books. How can they retain all that information? That's the age where they want to play and learn. I'm not saying children shouldn't learn to read books; of course, they should. But it should be enjoyable, and children should be allowed to discover their own personalities and interests.

2. BEGIN INTERNSHIPS SOONER

The typical internship begins when students are in their final two years of high school or when they graduate from high school. I believe they should begin sooner. I believe fourteen- or fifteen-year-olds are mature enough to learn about outside world. They should be working in summer jobs—not just being an assistant to a coach, for example, but working in a corporate environment or entrepreneurial environment. That will give them great experience. Let them explore the fun part of learning and figure out what they do and do not like sooner.

Selling lemonade in the summertime is a great learning experience for young people.

3. UPGRADE CLASSROOM LEARNING

Textbooks need to be more fun. I believe textbooks should contain practical work–life stories. Long, boring case studies don't cut it. Also, schools need to use video learning more.

At the beginning of 2020, when the COVID-19 pandemic began to sweep the world, the classes at many U.S. universities were proceeding normally. Then, in the middle of March, we were forced to take our classes completely virtual, as many schools were.

Moving to online learning, we had to be very creative. One of the challenges I faced was that I was just two weeks away from the midterm in one of my classes. That midterm exam usually consists of a quiz with multiple-choice questions, and students would come to the classroom to take it, while I monitored them. Obviously, we couldn't do that through a virtual screen, so I had to get creative. These are graduate students who are learning competitive strategy, integrated marketing, and leadership.

One day, I told the students, "For your midterm you will create a three- to five-minute video about leadership." I gave them a script to get them started, but I wanted them to convert that script into a three-minute video log.

Even though these are young people who are technologically savvy, many of them pushed back. They said, "We've never made videos in our lives. We don't know how."

But I wanted to challenge them. I said, "Well, it's a fun exercise."

Within a couple of days, I got feedback from them. They said, "Hey, I'm learning this. This is great." And within a week, I saw some phenomenal videos. The students converted my brief script on leadership into really nice videos with great music and unique effect. The class unanimously agreed that it was the most fun project they had worked on.

This creative outcome occurred as somewhat of an accident. The next semester, I was teaching that class partially online and partially in person. I had that class prepare videos also, and all the students agreed that it was a phenomenal assignment that led them to learn a new skill. It was an active, fun learning experience. They still have to read their textbook and study, but this time, they didn't have to memorize something from the book. Instead, they were allowed to learn while also discovering their own personalities and talents.

In my opinion, we need more of that type of learning going forward.

Creating videos is a practical, useful skill that students can use in the real world. In fact, many companies now require job candidates to submit videos as part of the interviewing and screening process. Job seekers can use a cloud-based recording platform like Loom to make a personalized video that they can provide links to on their résumés. And employers can use platforms like my Interview, a global video-interview service, to do all their candidate interviews live, via video.

Some of the students I teach have created sixty-second video résumés in which they share with prospective employers unique attributes about themselves. This helps job seekers stand out from the crowd; people enjoy watching these vlogs much more than they enjoy reading a paper summary of someone's life. Video is the future, and we need to build interactive video learning into our teaching.

4. MAKE LEARNING FUN WITH VIRTUAL ENGAGEMENT

Students are happy to come to colleges and universities, but many have come to appreciate the flexibility, efficiency, and convenience of remote learning. Once the COVID-19 pandemic forced many people to work and learn from their homes, we learned new ways to engage with people in a more cost-effective way. Some CEOs have decided to have their teams work remotely forever. Moving forward, interactive virtual learning has to be a part of our overall learning process.

5. FIND BETTER WAYS TO EVALUATE LEARNING

The grading system we have currently does not produce the desired results, in my opinion. The traditional way of testing students' knowledge is to teach them facts from a textbook. They memorize those facts so they can score high on their exams, and then they forget the facts at some point—often, the day after the exam. It's a boring process.

Grading is important, but there has to be a better way to evaluate learning. When instructors focus on grading, students ask, "Hey, is this going to be test?" If it's not, then they don't consider it important. They are focused more on making good grades than on learning. In my opinion, a grade should be based on combination of class participation, research-based learning, evaluative learning from the textbook and classes, and a heavy focus on group project they work throughout the semester.

6. TEACH REAL-LIFE SKILLS

There are many skills we need to learn in life that schools don't teach—for example, how to manage money, how to negotiate, and how to learn to respect people who are different from us.

In 2020, we saw social injustice up close every day in our communities and in the news. We watched as our nation struggled with issues related to DEI. Students experience all these issues inside and outside the classroom, but no one is talking about them in educational settings. People want and need to talk about these topics. Some people have strong opinions on these subjects but do not know the facts.

We need to have open conversations about important subjects like these so students are better prepared to face the real world.

HOW AI WILL TRANSFORM EDUCATION IN THE FUTURE

Whatever method we use to teach students, one challenge we face is that people learn differently and at different rates. Some students are more adept at "left brain" thinking with skills for analytical thought, whereas others are more skilled at "right brain" thinking with creative, literary, and communicative ability. Others are challenged in different ways with physical and mental disabilities, or skill sets that differ from one region of the world to another.

Ronald Schmelzer is Managing Partner and Principal Analyst at AI Focused Research and Advisory firm Cognilytica. He says one-way AI is transforming education is through AI systems being used to tailor and personalize learning for each individual student. Through the power of machine-learning-based *hyper-personalization*, AI systems are being used to develop a custom learning profile of each student and also customize the training materials for each student, based on his or her ability, preferred mode of learning, and experience.

By 2024, it is expected that forty-seven percent of learning-management tools will be enabled by AI capabilities. Rather than requiring teachers to create a single curriculum for all students, educators will have augmented intelligence assistance that provides a wide range of materials leveraging the same core curriculum but caters to the specific needs of each student.

Already, hyper-personalized and on-demand digital content is being created with the help of AI and machine learning. Big textbook providers now have their information broken down or condensed into smaller study guides, chapter summaries, flashcards, and "smart notes" for better reading and understanding. AI systems also have an online interactive interface that helps instructors see in which areas students need further assistance.

Increased use of AI to deliver education will help remedy the challenge of having too few instructors who are qualified to teach.

Think about telemedicine. Who could have thought, a few years ago, that we would have appointments with our doctors via a screen on our phones and computers or that medical specialists in urban areas would share their expertise with doctors and nurses in rural areas worldwide via telemedicine?

I believe education probably will experience a similar kind of evolution.

When the COVID-19 pandemic forced much of our learning out of the classroom, some students missed the face-to-face interactions they had in the classroom. This was true even for those students who are tech savvy. Even when AI transforms education, students will still want and need some sort of in-person interaction.

I believe there will always be significant value in great face-to-face learning led by qualified and passionate instructors. We should challenge them, but not completely replace them. After being involved in all teaching formats for the past fifteen years, I can comfortably say that nothing can beat a good face-to-face classroom lecture, where the students are being challenged in their critical thinking. That environment creates engagement and generates discussion beyond expectations.

That's how I feel now. Check back with me in ten years, and I might have a different opinion—because I'm adaptable.

WILL THE VALUE OF A FORMAL EDUCATION DIMINISH OVER TIME?

Whatever you need to learn, you can learn on Google. You can even learn how to ride a bike by searching for tips on Google and watching YouTube videos. You can go to Google to learn how to fix a computer, set up a sound bar, learn regression formulas, or anything else. So why would someone pay a lot of money and spend four years getting a formal college education?

The answer lies in the perceived value of that education. People attend reputable institutions because their degrees have value. The day we challenge that value is the day that higher education will be in big trouble. A college education from a highly respected university can cost hundreds of thousands of dollars, and you might spend half your lifetime paying back student loans. Now, formal education is obviously necessary in specialized fields like medicine and engineering. You need a medical education and degree to become a doctor. But to be a successful entrepreneur, do you really need an MBA? It might help, but the truth is probably not.

Instead of spending several years getting degrees, many people would prefer to spend that time starting their own companies or investing that money. Mark Zuckerberg quit college to launch Facebook, and now he is one of the wealthiest and influential people in the world.

You can be successful and learn life and save that money or invest that money. This is exactly what Mark Zuckerberg did. He didn't want to finish college and said "the idea is too good to waste and I'm going to start this company," and it became Facebook.

If educational institutions don't respond to people's needs and preferences, they will lose enrollment and therefore revenue. People will find alternative ways to become educated. What if Google University becomes a real university and offers education for free? It could happen. Anything could happen.

INNOVATION OFTEN OUTWEIGHS A COLLEGE DEGREE

Today, many organizations still prefer to hire candidates who have college degrees in certain roles. But that trend is diminishing. Imagine if a recruiter interviewed two people for a job. One had a traditional college degree. The other one says, "I don't have an education, but I just created a hedge fund that has generated returns of fifty-two percent in this down market."

The interviewer might say, "Wow, you're doing much better than my financial analysts, whom we are paying crazy money. How did you do that?"

The young candidate will explain how he or she wrote the program and refined it, and the CEO will naturally be impressed. Any company would invest in that kind of a talent. People invest in people. It's only a matter of time before the criteria we use to hire people evolves.

I have an MBA, but did anyone ever care that I have that degree? No. Did anyone ever ask me what my GPA was, or what subjects I studied? No. They just saw that I had the traditional degree and assumed what that might mean about my capabilities. That's the old way, and it's not going to go away tomorrow, but I think it will change eventually.

When recruiters interview candidates for positions in companies, they aren't interested in knowing what someone's role was; instead, they want to know what people *accomplished.* For that reason, I believe it will become less important whether or not someone has a college degree. If someone tells the recruiter, "I created an app that has four million followers," that's going to matter much more than completing a college degree. The CEO might say, "I don't want to hire you; I want to invest in, or buy, your company." Again, people invest in people.

Education is the biggest gift; how that education comes is debatable!

THE SUCCESS STORY OF INNOVATOR AND WHATSAPP FOUNDER JAN KOUM

Jan Koum, co-creator of the WhatsApp messaging service, says the idea for the company he launched with Brian Acton in 2009 came about so he could stop missing calls on his new iPhone. He got annoyed that he was missing calls when he went to the gym. So, he and Acton built an app that could let their friends know whether or not they were available, thanks to an easy-to-use feature called "Status."[4]

By 2014, WhatsApp had more than 400 million users globally. Ultimately, Facebook agreed to pay more than $19 billion to acquire WhatsApp, turning both of its founders into billionaires. In 2017, Koum and WhatsApp reached 1.3 billion monthly users.[5]

Koum's rise to success was meteoric.

He was born and raised in a small village outside of Kiev, Ukraine, the only child of a housewife and a construction manager who built hospitals and schools. His house had no hot water. As a young adult in America, he used food stamps to buy food. When he was only sixteen, Koum immigrated to Mountain View, California, with his mother. They got a small two-bedroom apartment through government assistance. His dad never made it over. Once in the United States, Koum swept the floor of a grocery store to help make ends meet, and his mother took up babysitting.[6]

He was a troublemaker in school, but by the age of eighteen, he had taught himself computer networking by buying manuals from a used bookstore and returning them when he was done. He enrolled at San Jose State University and moonlighted at Ernst & Young as a security tester. He met Acton in 1997.[7]

Koum didn't have a formal education, but he was an innovator. All over the world, people like Koum are learning how to succeed somewhere besides college classrooms.

The education system has remained stable and largely unchanged for many, many decades, but I think we will see major changes in the future as innovators enter the education space and use AI to transform education as we know it.

INNOVATION WILL DRIVE FUTURE DEVELOPMENTS IN EDUCATION

Who knows what the future holds? One day, Jeff Bezos of Amazon or a big conglomerate could enter the education industry and commercialize it according to their own business model. Jeff Bezos got into the media business when he purchased *The Washington Post* from the Graham family in 2013. More recently, he has launched a pharmacy. Who knows which industry he will get into next?

If Jeff Bezos or another successful entrepreneur does decide to invest in the educational field, it will be difficult for traditional educational institutions to compete with them. Entrepreneurs might discover that it's less expensive and more efficient to teach people through machine learning instead of having students go to the same classroom in person. I believe we can expect increased disruption in higher education, for better or worse.

4. "Jan Koum Got the Idea for $19 Billion WhatsApp After Missing Too Many iPhones Calls at the Gym," John Shinal, *CNBC*, January 19, 2018, https://www.cnbc.com/2018/01/19/how-jan-koum-got-the-idea-for-whatsapp.html.
5. Ibid.
6. "Exclusive: The Rags-To-Riches Tale Of How Jan Koum Built WhatsApp into Facebook's New $19 Billion Baby," Parmy Olson, *Forbes*, February 19, 2014, https://www.forbes.com/sites/parmyolson/2014/02/19/exclusive-inside-story-how-jan-koum-built-whatsapp-into-facebooks-new-19-billion-baby/?sh=7c7aa1cd2fa1.
7. Ibid.

I am not in favor of this. However, I believe education needs to be delivered by people who have the specialized knowledge and experience needed to deliver education to students effectively. Not just anyone can walk into it; that's why the current system has lasted so long and remains strong. We don't need to completely rewrite the whole code of education, but we do need to review and revisit the way we deliver it as the world changes.

Education is no longer a one-size-fits-all undertaking. When I teach blended courses, half of my students are 10,000 miles away from me. And if I'm teaching a class at 4:00 p.m. local time, then it's 4:00 a.m. time for them, and they have to get up early to get on the screen. Yes, it's a bit inconvenient for them, but I believe this is what the future of learning will be. University financial officers will realize that it doesn't make sense to pay exorbitant amounts of money to maintain classrooms when students can benefit from the flexibility of learning online.

We should not stifle creativity or innovation for the sake of convenience. We see the world from the lens that has been put in front of us until we are introduced to a new view. Curiosity always leads to creativity, in any learning environment. And innovation will drive the future of the educational system.

Again, I'm not against the traditional education system. I believe the United States has some of the best higher education institutions in the world. In fact, I am a big beneficiary of this education system. However, I truly believe there is a huge room for improvement. We need to be disrupted!

CORPORATE POLITICS

There are few things in life that can be termed as evil necessities and play a critical role in our professional growth, yet they are not taught anywhere else but the "University of Life". The corporate politics is the Wi-Fi Connection in professional life. No one is fully satisfied with it, but everyone needs it. For many, the corporate politics has been a rudimentary quintessential of professional growth since there has been a professional life. Everyone claims to dislike it, consider it dirty, condemn it and, yet become a part of it. Why? Because this is the nature of the beast.

It is a natural human behavior to compete with people on different dimensions. When we are not able to compete with someone on skill set and merit, our last resort and replacement for survival and growth is to strategize and divert our opponent's attention to undesirable activities. The best of the best fall prey to it and unwilling engage in it. This is a global phenomenon that exists in almost every company with more than one employee. There are many inept professionals who are amazingly adept in the art of corporate politics and make their way through managing up. While some may disagree with me, but I believe that professional growth because of soft-soaping often is short lived and carries the heavy baggage of damaged reputation.

The level of organizational politics may vary for an intern whose goal is to get an interview for a full-time position after the graduation compared to CEO of a Fortune company who is trying to gain control of the board of directors. However, the intensity increases as it goes higher up in the organization. So, what do we do about it? I guess, we may not be fully immune to it, but we can take a few steps to avoid a road full of corporate politics. It may take you a bit longer to get there but you will eventually arrive at your destination, and a bit more satisfied. Nothing beats earning a position!

Here are a few tips that may help.

1. Focus on your unique merit, skillset, and expertise
2. Identify your friends and foes immediately
3. Build a reputation of being transparent
4. Keep the daytime soap operas on your mind
5. Always keep your leadership informed
6. Develop a unique skill or expertise that no one has
7. Don't appear threatening
8. Choose your boss carefully
9. Always be valuable and become a necessity, even to those who play politics
10. Become an entrepreneur

The professional life is a sea where you must swim with Sharks. Build your career on your value where your leadership comes to you for a bigger role. Be ambitious but don't look ambitious. Make yourself a desirable talent for the competition and let your leadership know this with telling them. Make them feel that you are their competitive advantage. There may not be a cure for corporate politics but there are some treatments to keep it under control. Corporate politics needs a full chapter, and may be in my next book. For now, let's focus on other aspects of leadership.

SUMMARY

- We need to challenge the structured education system that was created hundreds of years ago. Today, the most successful students are usually the ones who are learning outside the classroom.
- People often mismatch themselves to their opportunities; we all need to follow our passions.
- Over time, we get weaker in some skills and stronger in others.
- Innovation will drive the future of the educational system.

QUOTES BY TARIQ KHAN

Leadership is seen, not claimed.

Every leader leaves a legacy; the one without a legacy leaves a poor legacy.

CHAPTER 9

Leadership from a Global Perspective

CHAPTER LEARNING OBJECTIVES

1. Understand the importance of learning and respecting how people in different cultures conduct business.
2. Learn how leaders can adopt a global perspective.
3. Explore a three-step diversity call to action for leaders.

"Global perspective" has become a buzz phrase in the past decade, as technology has closed the communication gaps that geographical distance once created.

But what is a global perspective, really? You don't have to have a business in every country or even travel to every country to have a global perspective. It really means widening your lens, so you view the world from the perspectives of people who are different from you. Our world is constantly changing. Even though COVID-19 has redefined our workplace and shifted our offices to our computer screens, we are still exposed to differing perspectives daily because of technology.

Imagine the first trip you took to a new city or a new country. You experienced sights, sounds, smells, and tastes that were much different than what you are accustomed to. You probably liked some of them and didn't care for others. But you probably appreciated learning how other people live and do things.

I believe it's important for all of us to explore other cultures and get to know people who are different from us. This is especially true for leaders. True leaders are not limited to their geographical or cultural boundaries, even if their businesses are domestic. It is critical to understand that we are living in a new world. People from different countries will be working *for* us, and we have to lead them. People with different perspectives will be working *with* us, and we have to engage them. Customers from different parts of the world will be doing business with us. We need to not only understand their cultures and styles but also cater to them. This is how companies and businesses will grow and expand their reach.

So just how can leaders adopt a global perspective?

EXPLORE NEW CULTURES WITH AN OPEN MIND

First, we cannot assume that people in other cultures do business the way we do.

Hilka Klinkenberg, founder of Etiquette International in New York City, says that less than twenty-five percent of U.S. business ventures abroad are successful. The main reason, she says, is "because Americans don't do their homework or because they think the rest of the world should do business the way they do business." She recommends doing extensive research on the country you want to do business in; learn communication styles, including body language; and take your own interpreter if you visit.[1]

Although the United States is considered a global superpower, it represents only four percent of the global population, according to the World and U.S. Population Clock.[2] If we limit ourselves to this bubble we know, we are ignoring ninety-five percent of the world population. No one can be an effective leader with such a limited worldview.

One of the main reasons the United States has achieved superpower status is because of our openness in embracing diversity and practicing inclusion. People from all over the world come here to realize their dreams, and this has been the vision of our leaders who have opened up this country to global commerce. We are truly a multicultural country. How many countries in the world you can think of that are the size of the United States and every third person is either Hispanic, Black, or Asian American?

The genesis of the United States was immigration. At one point, almost everyone in this country came from somewhere else. The myriad of Americans can trace back their roots outside this country, which is the Promised Land for immigrants. However, we must never undermine the hospitality of indigenous Americans who opened the doors for all of us.

We not only have a diversity of people but also embrace that diversity. However, *diversity* is just part of the equation, as mentioned earlier. *Inclusion* is the other important component. We must *include* people from other cultures in what we are doing and understand their perspectives.

China has the largest population of any country in the world.[3] Also, it has the potential to become the largest economy in the world. China's growth escalated because of the visionary leadership of Deng Xiaoping (1904–97).

As a Chinese communist leader, he was the most powerful figure in the People's Republic of China from the late 1970s until his death in 1997. He abandoned many orthodox communist doctrines and

1. "How to Take Your Company Global," *Entrepreneur*, https://www.entrepreneur.com/article/159252.
2. "World and US Population Clock," US Census Bureau, https://www.census.gov/popclock/world.
3. According to the US Census Bureau, as of July 1, 2020, China had 1.394 billion people, followed by India at 1.325 billion. The United States was a distant third, with a population of 330 million. See "US Census Bureau Current Population" at https://www.census.gov/popclock/print.php?component=counter&sec_ak_reference=18.e60fea5.1574146349.b558089.

attempted to incorporate elements of the free-enterprise system and other reforms into the Chinese economy.[4]

Deng Xiaoping was the main architect of China's economic growth. His perspective and leadership made China an economic giant. China has always been a large country, but before Deng Xiaoping's leadership, the country confined its growth within its own borders. Once China expanded its reach, the country became the economic giant it is today. According to the World Bank, the United States has 24.08 percent of the world's GDP, whereas China has 15.12 percent.[5] China is a manufacturing giant.

What is one of the most common written phrases in English? "Made in China."

WOMEN LEAD IN COMPLETING HIGHER EDUCATION

One of the most important and positive changes in the global work environment over time has been the growing role of women in business, which helps drive countries' economies. We still have a long way to go in this area, though. Although women have always represented about fifty percent of the world's population, they have never had the opportunity to be in the driver's seat.

In the second half of the twentieth century, there was a remarkable increase in the labor force participation rate of women. During that time, the U.S. economy experienced economic growth that increased the demand for labor. Baby boomers (those born between 1946 and 1964) began entering the labor force in large numbers in the early 1960s as they reached working age. Coupled with the rapidly increasing labor force participation rate of women, this resulted in a large influx of women into the labor market. After peaking in 1999, the labor force participation rate of women has continuously declined. The baby-boom generation has aged, and the economy experienced the impacts of the severe 2007–09 recession. The U.S. Bureau of Labor Statistics projects that women's labor force participation rate will continue its decline in the 2014–24 decade.[6]

In 2019, less than half (47.7 percent) of all women participated in the global labor force, a decrease from 50.9 percent in 1990. As for the share of women in the labor force in 2019, women represented thirty-nine percent of the worldwide labor force.[7]

But I still believe, again, that eventually, most of us will end up working for younger women who come from cultures different from our own. One fact that points to this future outcome is the increased number of women who are completing postgraduate degrees.

As of the first quarter of 2019, 29.5 million women in the labor force had at least a bachelor's degree, effectively matching the number of college-educated men in the workforce (29.3 million), according to

4. "Deng Xiaoping," *Britannica*, https://www.britannica.com/biography/Deng-Xiaoping.
5. "GDP by Country," worldometer, https://www.worldometers.info/gdp/gdp-by-country/.
6. "Women in the Workforce Before, During and After the Great Recession," Mitra Toossi and Teresa L. Morisi, July 2017, US Bureau of Labor Statistics, https://www.bls.gov/spotlight/2017/women-in-the-workforce-before-during-and-after-the-great-recession/pdf/women-in-the-workforce-before-during-and-after-the-great-recession.pdf.
7. "Women in the Workforce—Global: Quick Take," January 30, 2020, Catalyst, https://www.catalyst.org/research/women-in-the-workforce-global/.

the Pew Research Center. However, women have been a majority of college-educated adults for more than a decade. Women first received more than half the bachelor's degrees awarded in the 1981–82 academic year; today, they earn about fifty-seven percent of all bachelor's degrees. The number of college-educated women in the adult population (ages 25 and older) surpassed the number of college-educated men in 2007.[8]

Women now comprise nearly sixty percent of enrollment in universities and colleges. Fifty years ago, those gender proportions were reversed. The COVID-19 pandemic gave women an even bigger advantage in the educational arena. Enrollment in higher education overall fell 2.5 percent in the fall of 2020, compared to the fall of 2019. However, the decline among men was more than seven times as steep as the decline among women.[9]

Also, in 2018, women earned the majority of doctoral degrees for the tenth straight year, and women outnumbered men in graduate school 139 to 100. The Council of Graduate Schools reported that of the doctoral degrees earned in 2017–18, women completed fifty-seven percent of those degrees, and men completed forty-seven percent. Of the master's degrees earned in 2017–18, women completed 58.3 percent, and men completed 41.7 percent.[10]

A U.S. Department of Labor blog says, "According to Bureau of Labor Statistics data, in 2020, women's earnings were 82.3 percent of men's, and the gap is even wider for many women of color, though women only made 57 cents per dollar earned by men in 1973."[11]

How can we justify this?

We must do better, individually and collectively. Here is a diversity call to action for leaders:

1. Find out if there is a gender pay disparity in your company.
2. Reach out to your Chief People Officer and ask her/him to get it fixed in three years.
3. Make an announcement that there will be pay parity in your company in three years.

BUSINESS LEADERS MUST FOCUS ON DIVERSITY

Recently, my team gave a presentation on D&I to the CEO of a Fortune 500 company. I closed by saying that it is important for companies to mirror the diversity in America. The CEO said, "Well, we

8. "US Women Near Milestone in the College-Educated Labor Force," Richard Fry, Pew Research Center, June 20, 2019, https://www.pewresearch.org/fact-tank/2019/06/20/u-s-women-near-milestone-in-the-college-educated-labor-force/.
9. "The Pandemic Is Speeding Up the Mass Disappearance of Men from College," Jon Marcus, *The Hechinger Report,* January 19, 2021, https://hechingerreport.org/the-pandemic-is-speeding-up-the-mass-disappearance-of-men-from-college/.
10. "Women Earned Majority of Doctoral Degrees in 2018 for 10th Straight Year and Outnumber Men in Grad School 139 to 100," American Enterprise Institute (AEI) blog post, Mark J. Perry, October 8, 2019, https://www.aei.org/carpe-diem/women-earned-majority-of-doctoral-degrees-in-2018-for-10th-straight-year-and-outnumber-men-in-grad-school-139-to-100/.
11. "5 Facts About the State of the Gender Pay Gap," Janelle Jones, March 19, 2021, US Department of Labor Blog, https://blog.dol.gov/2021/03/19/5-facts-about-the-state-of-the-gender-pay-gap.

have a very simple principle. We hire the best people in the best companies. We practice diversity, but we don't have a separate focus on it. We consider diversity a part of our mainstream approach."

I acknowledged his comment and then replied, "Every third person in this country is either Hispanic, Black, or Asian. Every other person in this country is a woman. And millennials are now the largest living generation in America. We believe all these groups represent a diverse lifestyle and a culture. If your business strategy is not focusing on them, then you're leaving out seventy-six percent of the population, and that's not a good strategy."

To this CEO's credit, he immediately said, "OK, tell me more about it. What do you mean?"

I explained that, for a company to engage women, diverse races and ethnicities, and millennials doesn't mean that you hire only people in those groups. It does mean that leaders need to widen their horizons and understand how different people might prefer to do business. For example, if you're in the financial-planning business, it's important to understand that—and why—some women prefer to work with women financial planners. They believe women will understand their needs better than a man might.

Along those same lines, an Asian American might prefer to work with an Asian American financial advisor, and a millennial might connect more favorably with a millennial financial advisor. Now, this isn't always the case, but it's often true.

The face of America is constantly changing, and that has been one impetus for our growth. We cannot be confined to thinking that America is same as it was fifty years ago. Business leaders must understand that their employees, customers, and competition are likely to come from a different part of the world. And if you don't have a global perspective, you are putting yourself at a competitive disadvantage. No good leader in the world can afford to be at a competitive disadvantage.

HOW TO ADOPT A GLOBAL PERSPECTIVE

If you are a business leader who wants your company to achieve unlimited growth, then the first thing to do is to ask yourself, "How much do I want to grow?" Where you want to end up will determine the steps and the level of effort required to get you there.

Second, understand that your customers are exposed to a global marketplace. Even someone in a tiny rural community can use a computer or mobile device to gain access to products, services, and information across the globe. As a leader, no matter where you are, you can discover how Amazon, Alibaba, Google, and other businesses reach customers and do business globally.

Do you want to serve customers in the town or city you live in, the state, the country, or the globe? If your vision is to get global customers, then you have to have a global perspective, and you have to hire global talent. If you limit yourself to domestic exposure, you will not be able to serve your customers well, or as many customers. They will compare your products and services to companies that operate at a global level. Today, the world is your market.

Third, as you set out to hire a more diverse team in your company, strive to lead them in the most effective way possible by trying to understand their various cultures and values. By understanding, accepting, and celebrating their unique perspectives, you will be more likely to experience their best efforts.

With many companies working remotely because of COVID-19, it's easier than ever to hire people from different parts of the world. I am based in New York City, and I have an employee who lives in the Washington, DC, area. He has worked for me for eight years, but we have never met in person. Location no longer matters. It's no longer a barrier.

There are many different types of software, apps, and websites that provide services to businesses remotely. You can hire administrative, strategic, creative, and other services from all over the world.

LEARN HOW PEOPLE IN OTHER CULTURES DO BUSINESS

Adopting a global perspective is rewarding, but it can be unsettling at first. The way people interact with one another varies from one country to the next and from one continent to the next.

Recently, I traveled to Milan. When I arrived, I went to a currency-exchange counter to exchange some US dollars for euros. I asked the man behind the counter, "What is your conversion rate for one hundred US dollars?"

He stood up and said, "Calm down! Slow down. Are you from the US?"

I said, "Yes. What's wrong?"

He said, "Before you ask about the conversion rate, you need to say, 'How are you? How's everything?' And then you talk business."

I was kind of embarrassed, so I apologized and started over. I said, "How are you?"

He replied, "I'm fine. How are you?"

I said, "I'm fine, too." I paused.

He asked, "How can I help you?"

So, then I asked him about the currency-exchange rate.

Each of us is accustomed to doing things the way we learned to do them in the place we live. That is our perspective. But it's just one of many worldwide. In other parts of the world, people take long lunches and work less in the summer so they can spend more time with their families. Many countries offer more maternity and paternity leave. For example, in Finland, both parents can get up to seven months parental leave after the birth of a child. In Sweden, parents are entitled to paid parental leave for 480 days when a child is born or adopted. Besides Papua New Guinea, the United States is the only country with no national policy guaranteeing leave for new mothers. I call that poor leadership!

The best way to appreciate other cultures is to appreciate and understand them. In New York City, people tend to be adaptable, flexible, and accepting of other cultures. Failing to embrace other cultures will stifle your growth, creativity, and imagination.

DR. SHAILENDARA GHORPADE, PHD, RETIRED SENIOR EXECUTIVE, GLOBAL COMPANIES, GLOBAL ENTREPRENEUR

One leader who does a phenomenal job of acknowledging and embracing many cultures in his organization is Shailendra Ghorpade, an entrepreneur and retired senior executive from many global companies.

I have known Shailendra for nearly thirty years. I had an opportunity to work with him during my corporate days, and I consider him one of the sharpest minds in business. Shailendra has traveled globally and worked in several countries. I asked him what his advice is for leaders working with global teams. Here are the thoughts he shared:

Today's increasingly diverse workplace has placed new demands on its leaders. Managing a team of co-workers from different countries, or having the opportunity to work in other countries, creates additional hurdles for global executives who are faced with a workforce and work environment different from their experience at home. Unfamiliarity, distance, and a cultural divide produce an inherent trust deficit, on both sides, that needs to be overcome.

It begins with respect. And it is not just about avoiding disrespectful behavior, which is unfortunately the focus of many "diversity and inclusion" sensitivity training sessions. Making an effort to listen, not just hear, will lead to a better understanding of the diverse voices in the "room," helping facilitate respect for different points-of-view. Trust is tone-deaf without respect.

Managers instruct (from the "home office" handbook); leaders learn (from studying practices on the ground). Learning is an interdependent, social process that builds knowledge through engagement, mutual deference, and recognition—critical ingredients that can help bridge the trust deficit. Trust is built on knowledge.

To lead is to connect, not merely communicate. To listen is to speak. To learn is to engage and grow. Empathy, understanding, and recognition can help leaders communicate effectively and make the connections that earn confidence and respect. Trust is about making endearing connections.

Leaders in today's global workplace must listen, not just hear; learn, not just instruct; and connect, not just communicate, to be effective.

YOU DON'T NEED TO LIVE ABROAD TO DO BUSINESS ABROAD

Decades ago, if a company wanted to do business in Japan, they would have to travel to Japan, build an office or store there, and learn how to do business there. But today, you can offer your products and services in Japan without having to build infrastructure there (or anywhere else). If Amazon wants to do business in Japan, they don't necessarily need a full brick-and-mortar operation in Japan. All they need is a distribution system that enables them to deliver their products internationally.

Amazon is number one in customer satisfaction in the United States. Think about everything you have ordered from Amazon. Today, just about every household gets boxes delivered from Amazon. Their distribution system has become increasingly far-reaching. If Jeff Bezos had limited his perspective to domestic sales only, he probably wouldn't have become one of the richest people in the world.

There are 193 countries in the world. As of early 2021, I have traveled to about 55 of them, so there are 138 countries I have never been to. They are on my to-do list. Russia is one country I've never visited, but I'm constantly watching how the country is changing. After the breakup of the Soviet Union, I have often wondered how those now-independent states operate. Most of us don't have the luxury of visiting every country in the world. But we can read about them and experience them virtually. Also, because the United States is the world's economic leader and incredibly diverse, it's possible to interact with people from other countries and learn about their culture, traditions, values, and business practices.

When I started targeting diverse segments, one of the first markets I targeted was the Russian population in New York. We wanted to cater to them. I learned that there is a newspaper called *Novoe Ruskoe Slovo* that is written in the Russian language and caters to Russian Americans. That newspaper is over one hundred years old. Who would have thought there was a Russian newspaper in this country that is so old?

And then I learned that there is a huge population of Russians living in Brooklyn. In fact, more Russian-speaking Americans live in New York than in any other U.S. location. Around 1.6 million Russian-speaking people live in New York, New Jersey, and Connecticut. About 600,000 live in the city itself. According to the United States Census Bureau, in 2000, about six percent of the population of Brooklyn, one of the districts of New York, spoke Russian at home.[12]

Let's say I decided to do business in Russia. My business offers services, not products. So, the first thing I would do is to hire somebody who lives in the United States but has a Russian background. That person will understand the differences between the two countries. Also, it's likely that he or she still has some connections in that country.

You can expand your business anywhere in the world. To get started, hire someone who understands that culture, speaks that language, and understands how business is done there.

Similarly, the largest ethnic segment we have in the U.S. is Latin Americans. And when you look at this group, over 60 million people are of Latin origin, that's a huge population within the United States. And as you've seen, their impact from politics to businesses is huge and every company wants them to

12. "Where Do Russian Communities Live in the USA," Vladimir Yachmennikov, ForumDaily, February 1, 2017, https://www.forumdaily.com/en/samye-bolshie-russkie-obshhiny-v-ssha/.

be their consumer. And Univision and Telemundo, their television stations in the United States, are far bigger than many U.S. channels. So that clearly shows how our world is really becoming bigger without us going outside. We are catering to businesses all over the world. The iPhone that you use may be made in Taiwan or China, but we use it here. So, a lot of things really have changed in the last few years. And our workplaces become much wider. So as a business leader, you got to have a very global perspective.

During the COVID-19 pandemic that began globally in 2020, business leaders learned an important truth: we can do business virtually, anywhere in the world. There are new rules of engagement now. And that's great news because it means you can expand and grow with much less time, money, and effort than it would have taken ten years ago.

Ten years ago, most companies did not allow their employees to work remotely. If they did, it was on a limited basis—maybe one day per month, but now working remotely is becoming the norm. Being flexible and adaptable to change is a vital step in expanding your reach beyond your current capabilities. Visionary leaders will ask this important question: "How can we do businesses from a global perspective now, without having global locations?"

IN THE NEAR FUTURE, THE DEFAULT PERSPECTIVE WILL BE GLOBAL

NYU has one of the largest enrollments of international students in the world. The university's default perspective is a global perspective.

When I teach graduate students about leadership, we discuss integrated marketing and competitive strategy. In turn, they teach me how to have a global perspective. I am fortunate that I learn as much as I teach, and often more. In the future, I believe leaders will default to a global perspective because that is the only way to be competitive.

A few years ago, I was driving down the road. My wife was with me. Our son, who was young at the time, was sitting in the car with us. We had to stop because a big bus was parked right in the middle of the road. Apparently, it had broken down.

Our son asked, "What happened to the bus?"

My wife said, "Oh, it broke down."

Our son's response was, "Oh, no internet?"

At first, I didn't understand what he meant. But then I realized that his perspective was that if something breaks down and stops working, it's because people don't have the internet. I grew up at a time when the internet did not exist. Today, it's an essential part of our business. The next generation thinks that there was no world before the internet; everything works because of the internet.

Similarly, the next generation of leaders will think the only way to lead is through a global perspective. There are no boundaries to limit us, and if we want to grow, we must adopt a global perspective.

Talk to people from other cultures, people of a different gender than you, and people who are younger than you. Talk with your own children. It's likely that you will gain valuable insight into their different perspectives. The more perspectives you are exposed to, the greater your chances are for success.

SUMMARY

- You don't have to have a business in every country or even travel to every country to have a *global perspective*. It really means widening your lens, so you view the world from the perspectives of people who are different from you.
- Eventually, most of us will end up working for younger women who come from cultures different from our own. One fact that points to this future outcome is the increased number of women who are completing postgraduate degrees.
- Business leaders must understand that their employees, customers, and competition are likely to come from a different part of the world. And if you don't have a global perspective, you are putting yourself at a competitive disadvantage.
- If we limit ourselves to this bubble we know, we are ignoring ninety-five percent of the world population. No one can be an effective leader with such a limited worldview.

QUOTES BY TARIQ KHAN

Leadership is temporary, legacy is permanent.

Rich leaders have wealth of leadership.

CHAPTER 10

The Entrepreneur, the Leader, and the Coach

CHAPTER LEARNING OBJECTIVES

1. Learn six differences between leaders and entrepreneurs.
2. Understand the difference between coaching and mentoring.
3. Explore the benefits of taking a 360-degree leadership assessment.

Earlier in my career, I spent a lot of time in leadership roles at organizations in the corporate world. Then I felt a calling to take a route to entrepreneurship, and I launched my own company. So, I went from leadership to entrepreneurship.

I have seen others take the same route; I have also seen entrepreneurs become leaders. Both roles are quintessential for economic growth of any society, but, as mentioned earlier, they require much different skills. As I discuss later in this chapter, both entrepreneurs and leaders can benefit from coaching. Also, all entrepreneurs need to be leaders, but just being an entrepreneur doesn't make you a leader. You have to exercise leadership to be a leader.

Entrepreneurs and leaders are both visionary, but they achieve their visions in different ways. Many entrepreneurs are subject-matter experts in their fields. When Mark Zuckerberg cofounded Facebook, he did all the coding, just as Bill Gates built his own software products.

Leaders are often more process driven, so, while a leader might have a vision, he or she is more likely to focus on the process and to bring people to the team who have the skills needed to execute an idea. Effective leaders recognize which skills they lack, and they bring people to work for them who excel in those areas.

This is why leaders excel at improving companies that need improvement. They see where they could adjust processes and resources to optimize production. The goal of a leader is to leave an organization better than he or she found it. In contrast, the goal of an entrepreneur is to launch an idea.

Although entrepreneurs and leaders have many things in common, there are some significant differences. Let's look at those first, and then we will examine the traits of coaches.

DIFFERENCES BETWEEN ENTREPRENEURS AND LEADERS

The differences between entrepreneurs and leaders are subjective. Each person you ask will probably give you a different answer on this topic. Here are six differences I see between the two.

1. INNOVATION VERSUS EXECUTION

Entrepreneurs tend to be quite innovative. They are "hunters" with raw talent in many cases, and they have an unconditional passion for their ventures, along with a higher risk tolerance than most people. That's the DNA of an entrepreneur.

Leaders, on the other hand, tend to have stellar stewardship abilities. They have a passion to lead change in an effort to bring about significant improvement. They are great at finding resources and people to execute a vision for a successful company.

2. FLEXIBILITY VERSUS ADAPTABILITY

I consider entrepreneurs to be *flexible* and leaders to be *adaptable*.

For example, an entrepreneur can demonstrate flexibility in fulfilling various roles in his or her start-up company, working as the CEO, salesperson, accountant, IT manager, and janitor of the company. His or her ego will not be bruised while doing the menial tasks necessary to establish a strong foundation for the company. That entrepreneur will gladly knock-on doors and make cold calls to find an investor for the company.

Now, although leaders don't exhibit a great deal of flexibility, they do tend to *adapt* to changing circumstances. They believe in keeping an open mind and considering new ideas. They are not married to ideas; rather, they are married to the process. Many leaders are seen as custodians who are adaptable to circumstances.

For example, let's say a leader believes that his or her company should be making Product A, but a market analysis indicates that Product A doesn't have the potential for great success, given current market conditions. The leader will happily give up that idea or dream and pursue a product that promises to be more successful in the marketplace. An entrepreneur would more likely stay committed to the original idea. Entrepreneurs are flexible in aspects of their business ideas except for the ideas themselves.

3. GIVING DIRECTION VERSUS TAKING DIRECTION

Leaders set the standard for how business is conducted, and they set the rules of engagement with other people. They will take direction from a board of directors. They are willing to change their entire strategy based on the needs and demands of key stakeholders. They can be trusted to implement what is asked of them. They are committed to achieving or exceeding expected results.

Entrepreneurs, on the other hand, prefer to be the visionaries who drive the company's path forward.

Entrepreneurs judge their success through their own lens, not caring what others might think. They often challenge the status quo, and they are not ashamed to fail. They are independent and do not rely on others. They make decisions quickly, and they stand firm on those decisions. They follow their passion, regardless of what "experts" might tell them.

Leaders tend to be more sensitive about how the board, the marketplace, and customers are reacting. In contrast, entrepreneurs aren't afraid to engage in a power struggle with their boards of directors when there is lack of agreement over how to build the company.

4. BORN VERSUS BORN AND MADE

Another difference I see between the two is that entrepreneurs are born, whereas leaders are born *and* made. I believe that entrepreneurship is an innate trait—you either have it, or you don't. As for leadership, some leaders are born with leadership qualities, but if they're not, they can learn how to lead. Like in sports, they can get better through practice, working from some basic skills for that.

5. A FOCUS ON SUCCESS VERSUS A FOCUS ON PROFITABILITY

Many entrepreneurs struggle with financial management. I'm not saying they are not financially astute; many of them are. But they tend to be so focused on their vision for product or service development that they're willing to make some mistakes. They tend to be so driven by their passion and vision that they are not as committed to profitability as leaders might be.

6. DEVELOPING IDEAS VERSUS DEVELOPING PEOPLE

Entrepreneurs develop ideas, whereas leaders develop people.

An entrepreneur can be a one-person army, whereas a leader tends to depend on the team for success. Good leaders always select a good team, with each person contributing unique talents. They rely heavily on their teams to raise their odds of success.

BILL GATES: A LEADER *AND* ENTREPRENEUR

When we think of successful entrepreneurs, those who come to mind are the ultra-successful, such as Elon Musk, Jeff Bezos, Bill Gates, and Mark Zuckerberg. We all want to know how they achieved their success.

Bill Gates had a unique path to becoming one of the world's youngest billionaires. He is an example of someone who is both a leader and an entrepreneur. While most entrepreneurs' passion drives them to leadership, in his case, his leadership contributed to helping him discover his passion.

In 1976, Gates was twenty years old and preparing to make a big speech—the opening remarks at the First Annual World Altair Computer Convention in Albuquerque, New Mexico. He had taken a two-year leave of absence from being a student at Harvard University to form a computer software company with his high school friend, Paul Allen. That company eventually became Microsoft. Gates never finished his degree, although Harvard granted him an honorary degree in 2007.[1]

In 1994, he reflected on the early days of Microsoft. He said, "Microsoft was a business from the beginning, not that we had any clear view that it would ever be a large business. But I had to pay these friends I'd hired. At a minimum, I had to make enough money to pay their paycheck. And if I got enough confidence, we could sell a lot more. Then I'd be able to hire even more people to get ahead, to be the leader, and doing lots of products that could share code with each other and take the market." He says entrepreneurs need self-confidence to go out on a limb and try out new things. "Self-confidence is primary," he told the Australian Broadcasting Corporation, "and then finding your passion is an adventure."[2]

As of February 22, 2021, *Forbes* ranked Gates as the second-wealthiest person in the world, with a net worth of $123 billion. In mid-March 2020, Gates stepped down as a board member of Microsoft. He and his wife at that time, Melinda, chair the Bill & Melinda Gates Foundation, the world's largest private charitable foundation, which works to improve global health and create equal opportunity for people around the globe. As of early 2021, Gates has donated $35.8 billion worth of Microsoft stock to the Gates Foundation. In May 2020, the Gates Foundation said it would spend $300 million to fight the coronavirus pandemic, funding treatment, detection, and vaccines.[3]

While Gates's passion once was to build a software company, now his passion is to make a difference in the quality of life for people worldwide. His strong sense of entrepreneurship has enabled him to lead the type of life he wants to live while helping others. He is a prime example of how entrepreneurship can lead to an extremely self-fulfilling journey. He is not focused on profitability; he is focused on happiness by giving back.

I believe that entrepreneurs pursue happiness, whereas leaders pursue success.

---

1. "What Microsoft Billionaire Bill Gates Was Doing at 20 Years Old," Tom Huddleston Jr., MakeIt.com, updated April 9, 2018, https://www.cnbc.com/2018/03/29/what-microsoft-billionaire-bill-gates-was-doing-at-20-years-old.html.
2. Ibid.
3. "#2 Bill Gates, Real-Time Net Worth," Forbes, https://www.forbes.com/profile/bill-gates/?sh=6efe0cba689f.

COACHING VERSUS MENTORING

Coaching and mentoring are similar, but there are differences.

The International Coach Federation defines *coaching* as *"Partnering with clients in a thought-provoking and creative process that inspires them to maximize their personal and professional potential."*[4]

A simple, broad definition of *mentor* is "an experienced and trusted advisor." BusinessDictionary.com defines *mentoring* as an *"Employee training system under which a senior or more experienced individual (the mentor) is assigned to act as an advisor, counselor, or guide to a junior or trainee. The mentor is responsible for providing support to, and feedback on, the individual in his or her charge."* One note of clarification: while many organizations offer in-house mentoring programs, often as part of a leadership training program, it is common for mentees to work with mentors outside their organizations.

In my experience, coaching is more of a formal and structured relationship in which both parties have some "skin in the game." In other words, if I'm your coach and you fail, it's a reflection on me. Mentoring is more of a professional sharing of best practices and advice. If I'm your mentor and you fail, it's not really a reflection on me.

Also, coaching requires that the coach has expertise in the area in which the student or athlete wants to improve. If you want to improve at baseball, you will seek out a baseball coach, not a football or tennis coach. And if you want to excel in sales, you will choose to work with a coach who excels in helping people improve in that field.

Mentors, on the other hand, can have a broad range of expertise and provide general guidance to people in any field. They can listen to you as you describe your situation and then offer advice, based on their own knowledge and experience.

There was a time when coaching was something we heard about only in sports, not in business. When classic leadership was the norm, leaders had advisors to inform them about various aspects of their operations, but it was unheard of to have an ongoing coaching relationship with one trusted advisor. Many viewed it as a weakness to get help from someone else. But the opposite is true; failing to seek help is the true weakness.

A COACH SEES WHAT YOU CANNOT SEE

I mentor and coach many business leaders and entrepreneurs. One time, I was talking to an entrepreneur who was a prospective coaching client. He asked me a few questions about my company. He asked more questions about the size and revenue of my company than about my services. He asked why he should hire me when his company was bigger than mine.

I asked him, "Have you heard of Muhammad Ali?"

4. "Know the Difference Between Coaching and Mentoring," Kent State University, https://www.kent.edu/yourtrainingpartner/know-difference-between-coaching-and-mentoring.

"Of course," he said. "The greatest boxer of all time."

Then I asked him if he had heard of Michael Jordan, the greatest basketball player, and Serena Williams, the greatest tennis player.

He said, "Of course."

I asked him, "Do you agree that all of them were at the top of their game?"

He said yes.

Then I asked, "Did all these athletes have coaches?"

He said yes.

"Do you think their coaches were better athletes than them?"

He said no, and he understood my point.

I don't consider myself a great leader, but I know that, as a coach, I can identify mistakes or potential strategies a great leader might be missing. It's not those coaches are better athletes or better leaders than the people they are coaching; coaches' value is that they can pinpoint a path to improvement by sitting *outside* the fence, watching another person's performance through a different lens.

Coaches can identify details that others cannot see. We all have blind spots from our own vantage points; coaches can see beyond our blind spots.

So, a coach is not someone who is better than you. Instead, a coach is a trusted advisor who provides you guidance and a fresh perspective, looking at your business and situation from a different angle than you view it. Coaching is, basically, trust and guidance. It is a process of development and improvement coming from a trusted entity. Coaching works best when there is mutual respect, understanding, and commitment from both parties involved.

If someone refers you to a great coach, but you don't respect the coach for some reason, it will be difficult for you to trust that person and follow his or her guidance. And if the coach has no interest in your growth, then it will not be a beneficial relationship.

CONSIDER TAKING A 360-DEGREE ASSESSMENT

If you are not familiar with 360-degree assessments, you might want to take one. A 360-degree leadership assessment is a form of feedback for leaders in which their colleagues, employees, and superiors evaluate their skills, effectiveness, and influence. An important aspect of these evaluations is that they are anonymous. So, you will receive a report that summarizes your scores in certain areas, but that report will not identify how specific people evaluated you.

I have taken some of these assessments, and they are valuable up to a certain point. Once you receive your report of strengths and weaknesses, you are pretty much on your own in terms of figuring out how to make improvements.

The first step is discovering your roadblock; the second step is figuring out how to overcome it. Many leaders never implement the suggestions they receive. They say, "I'm going to get to that someday." And someday never comes.

This is why coaching is such an effective means of improving. Your coach covers both steps. He or she identifies what needs improvement and then helps you implement improvements in a way that's appropriate to your situation.

It's like exercise, nutrition, or physical therapy—although an expert can tell us what we need to do to improve, it's up to us to change our habits and processes on our own. But most of us are not good at implementing advice on our own. Your coach is like a physical therapist who will discover your weak points, watch you from the sidelines, and then talk with you about how to gain strength in that area. Your coach will always be there to help you. No matter how accomplished we are, we all need that kind of support.

EVERYONE NEEDS A COACH

In my opinion, every entrepreneur and every leader should have a coach. Your coach will see things you cannot see. He or she will discover what you are doing well and what could use improvement. Praise is great, but critiques are more important because they put you on a path to improvement. Feedback is critical to growth.

There are two times when you need a coach: first, when you are doing well and second, when you're not doing well. That means you *always* need a coach, or a mentor. The end goal is for your coach to lead you toward professional growth.

I have heard people say, "I am recognized as a global leader. I don't need a coach." But there is a life cycle to businesses; success can be cyclical. Someone who is number one today might be at the bottom of the heap next month. No one is the top for eternity.

It can be uncomfortable to have someone analyze, critique, and suggest improvements for something you are doing. It can feel like criticism, and some leaders take it personally. The hallmark of a great coach is to deliver suggestions in a positive, helpful manner and to avoid sounding critical. However, the hallmark of a great leader is to accept, consider, and act on feedback and critiques that are given with the intent of helping.

A big mistake that leaders or entrepreneurs make is defending the way they are doing things. Discussion is helpful, of course, but defending your position when your coach offers a suggestion is not conducive to learning.

People who say they do not need a coach are, basically, uncoachable. That is not a trait that defines leaders. In fact, coachability is one of the most desirable traits leaders look for when hiring talent.

When true leaders host town-hall meetings or listening tours, and when they solicit feedback from employees or team members, they listen intently. They don't defend their way of doing things. They ask a lot of questions and take notes. Most importantly, they *act* on the suggestions they hear.

From young people just starting their careers to Bill Gates, everyone needs a coach. Top athletes all have coaches; they don't get to the point one day where they no longer need coaching. They *always* need to improve. By the time you become a "veteran" in your sport or business, times will have changed. So, although you might have more experience than everyone else on your team, are you missing out on some skills that others have developed while you weren't looking? Or maybe the organization has changed, or the world has changed, and needs different skills from you than before.

Every one of us will *always* need a coach.

SUMMARY

- Effective leaders recognize which skills they lack, and they bring people to work for them who excel in those areas.
- Coaches can identify details that others cannot see. We all have blind spots from our own vantage points; coaches can see beyond our blind spots.
- Although an expert can tell us what we need to do to improve, it's up to us to change our habits and processes on our own. But most of us are not good at implementing advice on our own. Your coach is like a physical therapist who will discover your weak points, watch you from the sidelines, and then talk with you about how to gain strength in that area.
- *Coachability*—the willingness to hear and implement feedback for improving—is one of the most desirable traits leaders look for when hiring talent.

QUOTES BY TARIQ KHAN

Everything is, until it is not. So is leadership.

Knowing all about leadership doesn't necessarily make you a leader.

CHAPTER 11

Mentors Learn from Mentees, and We All May Work for Younger People

CHAPTER LEARNING OBJECTIVES

1. Explore five pieces of advice for younger colleagues who consider the old-school management environment to be foreign.
2. Learn five traits young people have today that give them a competitive advantage.
3. Understand the importance of having a mentor—and also of being a mentor to others.

Mentoring is a natural part of life; those who came before us often transfer their life experience and wisdom to us, and we do the same for those who come after us.

For many people, mentoring begins at home, with a smart uncle or aunt. They're the one you can always go to for advice about relationships, a repair your car needs, or a potential real estate deal. They know a little about a lot of things.

When I started my career, I didn't have such an uncle or aunt around me to look up to and go to for advice. I didn't have guidance, coaching, or mentorship when I was beginning my career. As I mentioned early in this book, my parents spent years in jail as political prisoners fighting for the restoration of democracy under military dictatorship, so my brother and I fended for ourselves. I know I would have benefited greatly from having that kind of support.

Each generation voices complaints about the former or next generation. This will always be the case. However, although there is no substitute for life experience, I believe that every new generation is smarter than previous generation. I am a Gen Xer, and I believe millennials are the smartest generation in history. They are the most technologically advanced generation, and I also believe they have given us far more than we have given them.

A YOUNG PERSON'S PERSPECTIVE CAN BE A CATALYST FOR CHANGE

When my daughter was a senior in college, I told her, "You should get an internship because that experience will help you find a job when you graduate next year. That's what companies look for."

She agreed to apply for an internship, and an insurance company offered her a paid summer internship. But, at twenty, in her last year of college, she was not excited about spending her summer working at an insurance company.

She went to work every day. At first, she described the work as "interesting." But toward the end of the summer, she saw the benefits of the experience. Almost at the end of her internship, all the interns were invited to a meeting with a senior executive to share their experience. In that meeting, the interns had asked her to talk about their experience in the internship and to describe what they had learned.

My daughter told them, "When I came to work here, I knew nothing about insurance, and I never really considered insurance as an important product. Now, after doing my internship, I have learned that insurance is among the most useful products. In fact, the concept of insurance is quite simple, but the insurance companies have made it complicated and unattractive. The smartphone, on the other hand, is quite complicated. Yet Apple has simplified it and made it attractive. Everyone needs insurance, but no one wants it. And most people don't need a new iPhone every year, but we all want it." The summer internship was a truly valuable experience for her and it led her start her career in the financial services industry, by choice.

Her comment summarized decades—centuries, actually—of difficulties insurance companies have experienced in convincing people they need to buy protection products. She saw the issue from a completely different perspective, and it was illuminating—and valuable. The company has begun making changes to its classic method of promoting the benefits of life insurance to potential customers.

Often, a young person's fresh perspective is just the catalyst we need to jump-start a project or business.

VALUABLE TRAITS YOUNG PEOPLE HAVE TO OFFER

Life has been simplified for young people, largely because of technology. Information is easily accessible, and they have access to resources they can use to simplify and innovate.

When I was in college and needed to look up some information, I would go to the library and search for the right books in the card catalogue—small drawers containing note cards that indicated where in the library stacks I could find various books. After much searching, sometimes I would discover that the book I wanted wasn't available; someone else had checked it out. So, I would have to ask the librarian to put my name on a list and call me when the book came in. Maybe a week later, I would get the call, and I would go back to the library to check out the book.

Today, we can get the answer to any question in a few seconds. Hint, google it!

When you have access to information, it makes you more resourceful, which gives you more confidence. It also makes you more competitive. The following are five traits young people have today that give them a competitive advantage:

1. **Innovation.** When you have instant access to information, you can spend your brain power and energy on creating something and being innovative. Many of the companies that are emerging as leaders today are the results of innovative young people coming up with unique products and services like Facebook, Google, Airbnb, Uber, Tesla, Spotify, and more.

2. **Fearlessness.** In my generation and those before it, we were expected to get a stable, full-time job at a company once we graduated from college. Failure was not an option. Today, failure is a requirement. We learn more from our failures than our successes, and young people seem to be more fearless than their predecessors. They are not afraid of failure. They realize that failures help them become stronger, and they expect to fail many times before they succeed.

   Many young people today accept jobs at companies and quit three months later because they don't like the work or the environment. They are much more confident than I was at their age. And confidence is a requirement for leadership.

3. **Education.** According to a 2019 Pew Research Center study, thirty-nine percent of millennials aged 25 to 37 had a bachelor's degree or higher, compared with just one-quarter of Baby Boomers and twenty-nine percent of Gen Xers when they were the same age.[1]

4. **A devotion to causes.** Young people today tend to be drawn to industries and companies whose values align with their own. They want to work with people who are passionate about the same causes they care about.

   Older generations sought to work for companies and brands that were well known and well established. When I graduated from college, I was determined to work for a Fortune 50 company. But today, young people are happy to join a start-up working out of someone's garage if that company is devoted to a cause they embrace. They are not nearly as brand driven as people my age were at their age.

5. **A natural adaptation to D&I.** Young people embrace D&I better than any other generation. They tend to be more color-neutral than their predecessors. They have grown up with more diversity on their playgrounds, on their school campuses, and in their everyday lives. They don't define people by their race, ethnicity, or gender. They don't have to *try* to achieve D&I like many in previous generations do. When I went to college, there were two genders—male and female. According to Healthline, today, there are at least 64 terms that describe gender identity and expression.[2] Many colleges have self-identified about 37 plus or 64 genders. Young people are more accepting of people who are different from them.

These five traits make me highly optimistic about the potential of our younger generations.

1. "Millennial Life: How Young Adulthood Today Compares with Prior Generations," Kristen Bialik and Richard Fry, Pew Research Center, January 30, 2019, https://www.pewresearch.org/social-trends/2019/02/14/millennial-life-how-young-adulthood-today-compares-with-prior-generations-2/.
2. "64 Terms That Describe Gender Identity and Expression," Healthline, https://www.healthline.com/health/different-genders.

MENTORS LEARN FROM MENTEES

Often, we learn more from our mentees than we teach them.

I constantly learn from my children, my students, and my mentees. In the old days, you were only supposed to learn from your elders—your parents, teachers, and coaches.

When people first began texting on their phones, I told my children they had to text to me using full sentences! They would use abbreviations and shortened words. Guess who adapted? I did. They wanted to simplify things, so they did. They told me, "Dad, this isn't grammar class." They were right.

Also, I objected to my son and daughter spending a lot of time on their devices when they first got them. But one day, my son asked me, "Dad, when you were young, did your parents tell you not to watch TV?"

I said, "Yeah, they did."

He asked, "Were they wrong?"

I replied, "Well, come to think about it, television is a source of entertainment and knowledge."

His point was clear: devices are just TVs with smaller screens; they give us access to valuable knowledge and entertainment.

I can say confidently that a lot of my learning comes from the next generation. Sometimes, when I have leadership challenges in my business, I will put up a case study in my classroom and ask the students, "How would you solve it?" Ten out of ten times, they come up with more innovative ideas than I would have.

If you have been reluctant to learn from those younger than you in the past, just try an experiment. Present a problem that needs to be solved to young people. You might be surprised at how easily and creatively they can solve it.

WHAT YOUNGER PEOPLE CAN LEARN FROM US

Now, although I am singing the praises of our younger generations, they still have some things to learn from those of us who came before them. Here are five pieces of advice I have for my younger colleagues who consider the old-school management environment to be foreign.

1. **Learn about financial management.** Often, in their excitement about starting companies they're passionate about, they fail to do their financial due diligence. They need to have a solid understanding of the monetization principles that will help their businesses thrive and grow. As I've mentioned, many start-ups have become successful, despite making no profits during their first few years in business. But why put yourself through that if you can avoid it?

2. **Increase human interaction.** We cannot do this again until we have conquered COVID-19. But once we get past the pandemic, I encourage young people to strengthen their people skills. Often,

when I meet younger people, I notice that they often avoid making eye contact, shaking hands, and following other traditional protocols of in-person interaction. I believe the pandemic worsened this lack of skills in face-to-face interactions.

3. **Take notes, but not in a distracting way.** Many young people take their devices into meetings and focus on them while others are speaking. Maybe they are taking notes, but maybe they're doing something unrelated to work. As the instructor, it's distracting for me when students focus on their devices because it appears to me that they are not paying attention. I prefer that they take mental notes or write notes on paper.

   This sounds old-fashioned, and it is. However, young people need to recognize that venture capitalists, board members, shareholders, and other people they need to make favorable impressions with are older people who abide by the accepted social protocols of the past.

4. **Dress appropriately.** Dressing casually is great, and I love it myself, but I think we are getting carried away. Many younger people wear sneakers and hoodies to work. I recommend dressing appropriately for your audience and for the occasion. If you don't have a suit and nice shoes, buy them. And when your shoes need shining, shine them! Yeah, they need shinning and cleaning too.

   People in my age group, especially those who worked in the Financial District and Wall Street, used to wear suits. Many of our best conversation took place at the shoe-shining stands in New York City. As a result, older people tend to notice the shoes other people wear. It makes an unfavorable impression on them if someone is wearing shoes that are scuffed and in bad need of a shine.

5. **Be patient.** I'm not saying you have to wait thirty years to become the CEO of someone else's company, like people did when I began my career. But if you work for someone else, recognize that you will be required to work your way up. Follow the career path and "pay your dues."

ACCEPT THE INEVITABLE PROGRESS WE'RE MAKING

As I mentioned earlier, I believe that someday, it may be common to see more women leaders in the C-Suites then men. While it may take a long time but then there are many things that I am now witnessing sooner than I expected.

I believe women are the leaders of the future, but women are still experiencing a pay gap in the workplace. In 2021, the National Partnership for Women and Families reported that, overall, women in the United States were paid 82 cents for every dollar paid to men.[3]

This is not acceptable.

In 2020, Kamala Harris, a multicultural woman born in 1964, was elected vice president of the United States. That historic occurrence is just the beginning. Whatever generation we represent, we need to

3. "America's Women and the Wage Gap," National Partnership for Women and Families, March 2021, https://www.nationalpartnership.org/our-work/resources/economic-justice/fair-pay/americas-women-and-the-wage-gap.pdf.

prepare ourselves to start interacting and working with younger women from various cultures who will lead us in the future. I believe this will be a positive change.

Tradition dies hard. Old habits die hard. But to adapt to change, and evolve, we must accept the shifts that are happening around us, in terms of demographics, technology, and mindset.

SUMMARY

- Often, a young person's fresh perspective is just the catalyst we need to jump-start a project or business.
- When you have access to information, it makes you more resourceful, which gives you more confidence. It also makes you more competitive.
- In the old days, we were only supposed to learn from your elders—our parents, teachers, and coaches. But today, we often learn more from our mentees than we teach them.
- Someday, it will be common for people to work for multicultural women who are younger than they are.
- It is unacceptable that women are still experiencing a pay gap in the workforce. As leaders, we must change this.

QUOTES BY TARIQ KHAN

Stupidity takes away many things, but it gives you an unconditional confidence of being right when you are wrong.

There are two types of leaders, those who make an impact and those who wish they did.

IN REMEMBRANCE

We acknowledge the many contributions to leadership that Mr. Michael Fung made to the business community during his career. He provided an interview for this book before his death in February 2021. Mr. Fung was a member of the prestigious Committee of 100 and a board member of five top-ranked companies. He served in many leadership roles at Fortune 500 companies.

MICHAEL FUNG

The world lost a leader, and I lost a friend.

ABOUT MICHAEL FUNG

Mr. Fung retired after 11 years at Walmart where he served as a senior vice president, both for global procurement and internal audit, and as the CFO for Walmart U.S. In that role, he was responsible for U.S. finance operations, e-commerce, and financial planning analysis. During his career at Walmart, Mr. Fung led the creation of Walmart's sourcing operations worldwide in addition to determining and establishing the legal entity structure in China post WTO. Mr. Fung also led the development and execution of Sarbanes Oxley procedures worldwide at Walmart. During his tenure as CFO, he transformed the finance team from transaction-based procedures to strategic finance, enabling the business to increase comp sales, market share, profitability and return on invested capital. Strategic Planning was transferred to U.S. Finance during Mr. Fung's leadership. Mr. Fung also led the implementation of SAP within the U.S. business during his management.

Prior to joining Walmart, he began his career with Deloitte in Chicago. He served as vice president and corporate controller for Beatrice Companies; CFO for Bass Pro Shops; CFO of Vanstar Corporation, a computer reseller and network integrator; CFO of Sensient Technologies (formerly Universal Foods Co.) a global manufacturer of colors, flavors and fragrances; and, after retirement from Walmart, served as interim CFO for Neiman Marcus and JCPenney. Mr. Fung served on the board of directors for Franklin Covey, Salt Lake City; 99 Cents Only Stores in Los Angeles; Floor and Decor in Atlanta, among others.

Mr. Fung was a member of the Financial Executives Institute and the American Institute of Certified Public Accountants. In addition to the boards noted previously, he was a board member and chair of the Asian Pacific Islander American Scholarship Fund, and a member of the Committee of 100, Ascend, OCA and the University of Illinois Foundation. Mr. Fung previously served on the UIC Business Dean's Advisory Council for more than eight years and on the Board of the University of Arkansas Veteran Resource Information Center.

In his keynote address at the UIC Business virtual spring commencement ceremony in 2020, Mr. Fung ended his remarks by stating, "Always be humble and kind," his favorite saying and one he embodied in his career and service to UIC Business.

CHAPTER 12

C-Suite Perspectives

Earlier, I mentioned how valuable experience is in shepherding an organization from a familiar position in the marketplace to a new reality shaped by unprecedented change. I interviewed four high-level, long-term CEOs in different industries to get their perspectives on leadership during changing times. The following are highlights from those interviews.

C-SUITE PERSPECTIVE: MICHAEL FUNG

Michael Fung
Former Senior VP and CFO, Walmart US
Former Interim CFO, JCPenney
Former Interim COO and CFO, Neiman Marcus
Former CFO, Bass Pro Shops

Throughout my career, I've worked at small, medium, and large companies. Although difficult to rank in priority order, there are some characteristics and attributes that are similar among successful leaders. Below are just nine of the key traits I believe effective leaders must have.

NINE ESSENTIAL ELEMENTS OF EFFECTIVE LEADERSHIP

1. **Humility**—In a commencement speech I gave, I talked about the lyrics of a country song called "Always Be Humble and Kind." Humility is a difficult quality to keep in check because over time, we think we know everything. We're successful, and we can do no wrong. Nonetheless, a leader has to be humble. Don't let your ego get in the way.

2. **A Vision or Plan**—Certainly, in the Fortune 100 companies—and even at smaller ones—you have to have a sense of vision or a plan, as well as the ability to prioritize with that plan. We did some truly earth-shattering things with far-reaching initiatives at Walmart, and at times, the team didn't understand how to get there. What I had to do to achieve our longer range plan was to create an intermediary phase in which we laid out the A-to-B steps that needed to be accomplished.

3. **Execution of that Plan**—The ability to execute is also important for leaders and their teams. Throughout my career, I've had the ability to execute and get things done. Walmart promoted a "ready, aim, fire" mentality that emphasized beginning the task, learning along the way, and making mid-course corrections rather than analyzing everything and trying to execute it perfectly.

4. **Attaining Success and Momentum**—In consulting, it's always about little successes because that's how you build the credibility to tackle more arduous or far-reaching tasks. But you have to be successful in something because the team has to believe in you and in themselves.

5. **Selflessness and Shared Hardships**—Many of us on the API Board came from nothing—we had mid-to-lower-class upbringings in which we went through the trenches and earned everything ourselves. We understand the plight of those who have tried to move up through society, having shared that experience. That sense of selflessness, humility, and shared hardship with your team is critical to solid leadership.

6. **Excellent Communication Skills**—How a leader is perceived by his or her organization is really important, especially to members of the team. Excellent communication skills, both written and oral, are a must, as well as emotional intelligence and a sense of empathy for the team and for the organization.

7. **The Ability to Manage in Every Direction**—Similar to having emotional intelligence is the ability to manage up, down, and throughout the organization. In very large organizations, there tend to be political fiefdoms and other points of tension to deal with. Teams look to their leaders to help bridge those experiences and build up allies.

8. **Good Decision-Making Skills**—You can't always have consensus, so it's also important to be good at decision-making. The worst outcomes result from overanalyzing things, being unwilling to take a chance, and ending up on the defensive. Your team will pick up on that very quickly, as will your business partner. In essence, be willing to take a risk, go forward, and stand for something.

9. **Optimism**—Finally, my time in the military taught me that a leader needs to have an optimistic, can-do attitude. You have to be able to overcome overwhelming odds, negative perceptions, and naysayers. Military people are willing to take on incredible odds because they believe in you, in the

task, or in the mission at hand. Lead the team. Inspire confidence that you will achieve success. Be accountable, make a decision, move forward, and simply accomplish it.

INVEST IN, UPLIFT, AND EVOLVE YOUR TEAM

You have to have a great team. As a leader, it's up to you to determine who should be on that team. Who are the team members, and which roles should they fill? Taking responsibility for your team is a chief aspect of leadership. Along with that, it's essential to ensure that you trust your team members and that they trust in you.

Don't ask your team to do something you're not willing to do. Be there at all hours with them to the extent it's possible, whether it's over the holidays or anything else. If you don't have kids, step in for your team members and do some of the work yourself. Make sure that they're able to enjoy quality time with their families.

Developing individual team members is also important. It's all about the critical insights—getting real and giving constructive criticism. Although most people don't like giving constructive criticism, we as leaders need to recognize that it's our gift. Your job is to develop your team members so that they can flourish anywhere, not just within your organization.

At Walmart, we provided more finance VPs than the rest of similar organizations combined because we were willing to find the best talent, develop them, and challenge them. Then, if they wanted to do mergers and acquisitions (M&A) or go to other businesses, we let them do that. As a result, we created a virtuous cycle in which the best people wanted to come work for our organization.

We also used the term "servant leadership" at Walmart a lot, which is the idea that your job is to help your team succeed. Whether it's dealing with resources, priorities, or vision, it's a leader's duty to encourage his or her team members and enable them to accomplish things.

LEVERAGE THE EXPERIENCE OF WELL-ESTABLISHED LEADERS AND BUSINESSES

Although new leaders are incredibly bright, visionary, and technologically adept, many of them have a shorter horizon in sight.

One of their weaknesses is that they haven't experienced enough business cycles from the ground up, working through the various disciplines and processes. Although they're visionary, they may not know how to improve operating excellence in a supply chain or how to improve something in operations. Senior leaders have actually done a lot of these jobs and therefore know what it takes. They've worked in those functional areas, gone through product development, and seen business cycles in their entirety.

New leaders will have to make sure that they have expertise within their teams, so they know how certain things are done at the ground-floor level. At the same time, they'll have to leverage their own skills and knowledge in the areas they have expertise in.

When young people say they want to join a start-up, I advise against it. At a start-up, there's no one to teach you, mentor you, or train you. You're going to do it all from the seat of your pants, even though you don't know anything about the business. If you have the chance to develop those skill sets at a big or midsize company, you go much deeper. They have the dollars, the experience, a better sense of customer segments, and an overall knowledge of what to do. In essence, you can learn more from well-established companies than from a start-up.

We haven't had a business recession in a long time. As a result, a lot of start-up enterprises and early-stage companies have never experienced one before. We've all seen the dot-com boom and bust. What we have now is direct-to-consumer companies that are just burning through cash. If your start-up flamed out and went bankrupt, what did you really learn, other than how to spend a bunch of cash? Furthermore, it can be hard to get back into a bigger company once you've fallen off the hierarchy of leadership and development.

I still believe my old finance courses, which taught that ultimately, your share price is the present value of discounted cash flow in your enterprise. If it's just burning cash, your company shouldn't be listed and have a valuation. Just because a brand is established doesn't mean it's successful. You have to get to profitability.

RESIST THE PREVAILING WISDOM OF OPTIMIZATION

As a modern-day leader, it's essential to be brave, original, and disruptive. The fragmentation of customers is so much more pronounced today and reaching them is more difficult than ever. You have to innovate in today's environment and be willing to incur additional costs because doing so results in greater flexibility.

Those of us from a finance background have always focused on optimizing the supply chain, optimizing how we source, and optimizing store operations. It's been all about leading at the lowest possible cost to improve profitability. What COVID-19 and the current environment have shown us is that it's good *not* to optimize your supply chain. While it used to be that no one could predict "black swan events"—unpredictable events that are beyond what we might expect of a situation and that have potentially severe consequences—we've had more black swan events in the past ten to twenty years than seems imaginable. Whether a pandemic, a major earthquake, or terrorism on a global scale, people have to plan for the future even more than before.

For that reason, leaders have to resist the prevailing wisdom of optimization. It's not necessary to have the fastest product to market or the greatest productivity per reach of advertising dollar. Instead, ensure that you truly understand present-day risks. Diversify your sourcing of critical raw materials and products from various countries.

FOCUS ON CORE STRENGTHS AND VALUES, AS OPPOSED TO FINANCIAL MANAGEMENT

Although this may seem contrary, I believe strong financial-management experience isn't absolutely critical for a C-suite leader to do well in his or her role. Understanding what the value drivers are in the business is typically more important than focusing on strong financial management.

A lot of CEOs and COOs aren't necessarily CFOs. Even if they have a finance or accounting course in their backgrounds, their expertise is in tweaking the levers that achieve operating excellence, deliver profitability, and increase the company's value.

Obviously, financial information is business data and shows results. Therefore, an understanding of finance is necessary to some extent, but it's not essential to know technical details, capital markets, or activity-based costing. You certainly don't need to know anything about financial reporting or what auditors do. In a leadership role, what you really need to understand are the drivers of value or points of differentiation that your company has. Focus on the core strengths of your business, whether they are in the supply chain, merchandising, or operations.

For CFOs specifically, having expertise in the main functions of what a CFO does is key. Core skills to ensure the firm's survival and access to capital are essential, as well as the ability to step up quickly and take control when the company needs you.

What's been happening to CFOs is that instead of being financial-reporting gurus, they become strategists. They actually act as operating people with an understanding of the multidisciplinary functions and interactions among the group within a company. In essence, they're the right-hand people to the CEO. They have the duty and privilege of telling the CEO what he or she needs to know about what's happening in the business. Simultaneously, they address the costs that are being embedded or incurred—and that may not be necessary.

More than anything, however, CFOs need broader operating experience and a real understanding of the key drivers of the business. Financial expertise is always going to be required, but companies need more of a general manager going forward, as opposed to a technical expert who excels only in finance functions.

MINE IDEAS FROM A DIVERSE COLLECTIVE

It's clear that diverse teams and boards lead to stronger performance and greater profitability. Rather than addressing D&I as a separate function, leaders need to embed it into company culture. It should be core to its success and to the development of its leaders, including how they understand their customer segments. It's incumbent upon the D&I leaders—and also the operating leaders—to ingrain and incorporate it so it becomes seamless, instead of being an add-on program or project.

In the past, many older leaders worked their way through a lot of functional disciplines, but future leaders are coming from all sectors on a global basis. Therefore, to be truly successful, it is essential to mine ideas from a diverse collective. Only through true team involvement and engagement from all parties will there be speed of thought, innovation, and execution.

A diverse and inclusive environment is crucial because that's what your customer base is. Not only is it what's expected of society, but it also produces results. In the end, results are how businesses measure results, so D&I will have to operate smoothly.

RECOGNIZE THE HOLISTIC VALUE OF PHILANTHROPIC ENDEAVORS

When you, as a leader, are actively involved in nonprofit organizations, you actually walk the talk. If you are really vested in the community and in the development of people, then you're also interested in the development and care of people who are less fortunate and need assistance. Giving my time to philanthropic activities made me a better manager and leader. It taught me what my customers were experiencing—what they dealt with on a day-to-day basis.

My philanthropic engagements not only ensured that I understood our customers more but also helped me identify potential board members for the boards I'd sit on in the future. Not all prospective board members will come from places you've worked at previously. Having the chance to see other business leaders engaged in philanthropy allows you to determine who walks the talk of a true leader. The last thing anyone needs is somebody on the board of a nonprofit who's very successful in business but is not actually willing to do any work on a nonprofit.

That's why it's so important to appreciate the program people at nonprofits. Realize that it's up to you to work with them. Use your network to make the nonprofit successful. Although your volunteer service may grant you access to company resources and donation dollars, it's not about name recognition. Rather, you learn a lot about other people, your network, and yourself.

COME TO TERMS WITH THE FUTURE OF RETAIL, AND INNOVATE BEYOND IT

It's a misconception among consumers that internet sales are profitable for companies. When Amazon first came out and Walmart studied it, we thought that internet selling companies like Amazon would get up to ten percent of total retail sales. Now, internet sales are probably twenty-five percent of total retail sales, although it can go up in some particular quarters because of brick and mortars shutting down.

When Walmart studied Amazon twenty years ago, we discovered that Amazon didn't make money on any item it bought, held as inventory, and resold to a customer. To this day, Walmart's e-commerce sales—which are worth more than $30 billion dollars—still don't turn a profit.

Take Caspar and its mattresses as the poster child of direct-to-consumer (DTC) brands. It's always been amazing to me that a customer would be willing to buy a mattress based only on advertising over the internet or email, without ever seeing it or trying it. Plus, a lot of extra costs are incurred along the way.

Once the mattress is ordered, it has to be shipped to someone's home. They have the option to try it for thirty, sixty, or ninety days free, and if they don't like it, they ship it back.

In the end, although Caspar enjoys brand-name recognition, they still don't make money. Walmart doesn't make any money on internet sales, and the same thing is true at Target. When there's greater price transparency, it squeezes markets. It's also standard to offer free shipping and returns. Even if you have in-store pickup, these additional costs are embedded. As a result, only the customer receives the benefits. That's why there is no profitability in internet sales.

There have simply been too many stores with an excess of "me too" type products that will inevitably fall by the wayside, their demise hastened by internet sales. B- and C-type malls, unlike the high-end, class-A malls with destination stores, are headed toward Armageddon. Whether it's Sears, JCPenney, Neiman Marcus, or Macy's, customers can now find the curated assortment, endless aisles, insight, and product analysis they once offered on the internet. There, purchases ship for free and arrive within two days. Shopping has been made so convenient that the demise of brick-and-mortar stores is easy to see.

In spite of that, a recent survey found that there *is* a social aspect to shopping. Brick and mortar stores will always exist to satisfy that, even if on a smaller scale. There may be a lot fewer than there are today, but if they can appeal to customers with the right products, presentation, and the experience of a store that can't quite be replicated on the internet, they'll find success. Mostly, what's at risk are those B- and C-type malls.

BE FLEXIBLE AND ADAPTABLE IN AN EVER-CHANGING WORLD

The future of teams and leadership was stressed as we learned how to work remotely with some degree of permanence due to COVID-19. Both from a leadership standpoint and a commercial one, we began to see huge changes play out.

The whole discussion about whether or not remote working is possible has been answered: yes, it's possible. Keeping us from it for a long time was the question of measuring productivity—are we as productive and profitable working remotely as we are when we work together, in person?

All of us have had a chance to walk down the hallway to a boss or a colleague's office to say, "Hey, can I bounce an idea off you? Hey, I need a quick decision on this." Or "Hey, can I take five minutes of your time?" Some of those interactions make up the most valuable time you can get. Having to schedule a Zoom call to talk to your CEO, your boss, or your colleague isn't a substitute for time spent face-to-face—that's irreplaceable.

Teams, as I mentioned, are about trust. Trust is built on individual relationships, whether that's getting coffee, having lunch together, or playing company softball. Walmart used to have what I called "war rooms." When there was a problem, we'd bring a multifunctional group in, and we wouldn't leave that conference room until the problem was solved. We'd whiteboard or blackboard the issues and go through all their aspects on a multifunctional level. The question from a management perspective is whether or not these processes are as effective using only technology.

Although we've all adapted and learned to use Zoom, Teams, or Duo, everybody uses them differently. Another issue with working from home is that there's a tendency to work much longer hours, even with the time gained from not having a commute. Also, during the COVID-19 crisis, whether it's kids or pets that interrupt, there's a whole laundry list of issues to deal with at home. On the business side, however, the need for real estate or open office space is certainly dwindling.

Again, it's all about the ability to be productive. When you have more than fifty people on a call, it's difficult to manage everybody effectively. In a Zoom room, you could have people who are shy and unwilling to speak up. They could skate by in Zoom calls forever, whereas in person, you as a leader can seek them out.

From a sales or commercial side that includes cold calling or convincing people on complex sales, Zoom by itself could be perceived as inadequate. It's a tool that can only go so far in connecting us as individuals. Trying to convince someone of the value of your firm or your D&I is more difficult without that in-person contact.

Technology also increases the risk of cyberthreats. I am not aware of any cybersecurity issues or major breaches so far, but that doesn't mean that they won't happen. It boils down to the use of technology, less office space, and whether or not it's possible to be as productive and as profitable remotely as face-to-face.

During COVID-19, the cleaning and disinfecting factors, as well as social distancing, had huge implications for various businesses. For example, individual counties in California could determine what the rules and regulations to operate a retail store would be. Even though all 99-cent stores sell similar types of products, each county could determine what was an essential item and what wasn't, as well as the hours that employees could and could not work. Although there are CDC guidelines, they're up to interpretation by each individual county. This makes it difficult to comply, in addition to bringing up liability issues that leaders needed to contend with.

All these things are workable, however. They have forced us to develop the necessary skills, on both a management and a commercial level.

C-SUITE PERSPECTIVE: DOUG HAMMOND

© D. Hammond

Doug Hammond, JD
CEO
National Financial Partners Corp. (NFP)

NFP was founded in 1999 to invest in insurance intermediaries, primarily in the life insurance space—a unique approach relative to what others had done in the same space. The idea of the business was to celebrate entrepreneurs, not by consolidating businesses or by creating a common operating structure but instead by allowing entrepreneurs to do what they do best.

BUILDING AROUND A COMMON MISSION AND THEME

We acquired close to three hundred businesses between 1999 and 2005. They all were operating independently under a holding-company structure. We took the company public in 2003 at $25 a share and continued with that strategy. I served as a counselor to the CEO of the company, and I was part of the executive team. Primarily, my function as the chief legal officer related to mergers and acquisitions, legal and regulatory compliance, and legal matters.

After we took the company public, our stock price increased to about $60 a share in 2006–07. Then came the recession, and our stock fell from $60 a share to just under a dollar. This happened over the course of about ten months. With this steep decline in the stock price, investors lost confidence. The company had a fair amount of debt on its books, and the recession affected certain aspects of our business significantly. At that point, the general view was that the company would ultimately go out of business.

But many of us on the management team had a different view. We had acquired great assets, and we knew the low stock price wasn't justified. The company's real crisis was a failure to align our assets and resources around a common theme and mission to serve clients in a broader and more comprehensive way. Our company structure was very decentralized and disparate, leaving the firms we had acquired to just do their own thing.

During the financial crisis, I gave up my title as general counsel and focused on the operating structure of the business as the chief operating officer. All the business units were reporting into me, providing a comprehensive view of what was working, and what wasn't, and how we needed to prioritize action.

Our leadership team had a clear vision of the quality of the company's assets and the opportunity to better integrate and grow them. We also had a group of assets that were not ideally suited for the transition. I envisioned that if we organized those assets in a certain way, we could create a tremendous amount of value—far greater than the $60-per-share value we achieved in 2007. We just needed to align the resources around a common mission and theme.

BELIEVE IN THE PLAN AND EACH OTHER

At that time, many people involved with the company were despondent, fearing that we were going out of business. We had issued stock to acquisitions at a price that had since dropped considerably, which created additional stress. There was a concern that if we couldn't turn things around relatively quickly, firms we had acquired, particularly the ones critical to our transition, would just walk away. It was important to lay out an inspirational vision for the business that we all believed in.

When I look back on it, I realize that our only "secret sauce" was that we communicated the vision passionately, aggressively, and consistently. We described our opportunity and what it would take to get where we wanted (and needed) to go. I truly believed we could achieve great things together if we aligned our resources and aligned our company around a common theme of serving our clients.

In order to make sure our clients were taken care of, we first needed to take care of our employees. We have consistently focused on making sure our employees felt appreciated and recognized, building a culture for our employees that we knew would create better outcomes for our clients.

I also knew we had developed the right roadmap and had the right people on the team ready to make it happen. In my mind, failure was not an option and I think that came through in how we articulated the vision.

COMMUNICATE YOUR VISION CLEARLY AND OFTEN

I learned that when you set out to accomplish something big, people want to tell you that you're wrong, and why. But if you continue to communicate and refine your communication in a way that's credible, by presenting the goals as achievable, people will begin to recognize that you know how to achieve success and you ultimately build consensus for the direction of the company. We shared the same message with everyone for six months, and then everybody was on the same page. We finally began to row in the same direction and execute toward a total restructuring and reorganization of our business. It was completely different from the themes we had when starting the business.

It was no longer about a decentralized operating structure. Now it was about a common brand and go-to-market strategy. It was about aligning all the complementary resources around client opportunities. It was about creating a common infrastructure and operating platform so we had transparency about our data. We understood what our business was, where we were strong, and where we needed to be stronger.

I also believe we succeeded because we were bold enough to identify which of the businesses we had acquired were not the right fit for where we were taking the company. We set out to transition assets that were not core to our new vision for the business. During that period of time, we sold off close to 100 of the firms we had acquired—not an easy task, especially with everything else we were trying to do—while preserving the best of what we had. It was not without its challenges, but we created value from that.

PIVOT BASED ON CIRCUMSTANCES; CHANGE DECISIONS WHEN NECESSARY

Tenacity is a critical ingredient for success—I definitely got that from my dad. He was a fighter pilot in World War II and a career military officer. He was a prisoner of war in Korea and an intelligence officer in French Indochina before the Vietnam War.

He taught me some good lessons as I grew up. One of them is that when you're at the top of the heap in terms of leadership, the decisions that end up on your desk don't have easy answers. As a result, leaders often are not certain about the decisions made, but it's still critical for leaders to state goals and make decisions that provide guidance to others. You want your team to follow you in a specific direction and that requires decisiveness. Most important, my father taught me to closely monitor the outcome of your decisions and be quick to pivot from a decision if you learn that it's not the right one.

You learn more and more as you execute toward the decision and learn quickly whether or not it's the right one. You can't hold onto things just because you've decided to do them a certain way. Remain flexible so you can pivot based on circumstances and shift in an alternate direction if you see the opportunities align in a different way. Then, the decision-making process becomes clearer when a bit of time passes. Some leaders view changing your mind as weakness, but I learned from my father, and have seen it throughout my career, that the real weakness is in refusing to pivot when you know you are no longer on the right path.

If you have little or no experience in a venture that seems to have potential, don't walk away from it just because you aren't one hundred percent sure about how to approach it. Just figure it out. Intellectual curiosity goes a long way—actively listen, ask questions, commit to learning. That's advice I received from a colleague of mine at a law firm I worked at early in my career.

I've always been fairly nimble in setting a goal and developing a plan of execution, and then monitoring progress. I like to revisit decisions along the way to ensure they're still the right ones. And when you're part of a team with aligned values and goals, there doesn't need to be ego in terms of how to get there, just as long as we do. That sometimes requires changing course.

I think it's important for leaders to acknowledge that the plan you had at the beginning of a project will likely change. It's not a failure or shortcoming. It's just that we learn as we move forward and recognize better ways to do things. Getting hung up on it isn't productive. Accept the need to adjust or refine and move on from it. Resilience and tenacity drive success.

There is a great example of this in our journey from IPO to going private. When NFP went public, the stock started at $25, went up to $60, and then back to just under a dollar. We recognized a need to change both our business model and our public company status. We took the company private in 2013 and I took over as CEO. We've done three recapitalizations since, creating significant value for stockholders and our capital partners. We recognized a need to change and saw an opportunity to go private. We're the company we are today because we checked our egos, focused on a plan, built a team of dedicated and talented people, and executed really well. And, we were never reluctant to pivot when we discovered that we were on the wrong path despite the best planning.

PROMOTE FROM WITHIN

I have also been a supporter of promoting people from the ranks of NFP as a first course of action when we need a leadership role filled. We want people within the company to know that those opportunities are there for them and that they can advance if they perform well, are creative, and work well and collaborate with others. This sends a clear message that talented people don't need to leave NFP to advance their careers, which is great for retention, culture, and results.

Some of the leaders we've brought into leadership positions from outside the company weren't the right fit. When people step into roles and start dictating and implementing changes without listening, that's a red flag. We want creative people with ideas and vision and ambition, but listening and learning are also important. Thinking you can do things based on your own plans without the buy in of the team or incorporating the thoughts of employees at all levels across the organization is one of the fastest ways to fail.

Recently, we brought in a group of leaders through an insurance brokerage we acquired. I always advise leaders new to a company to go through a "honeymoon period." At first, they don't have a ton of responsibilities because they haven't yet integrated themselves into the day-to-day operations of the business or earned the trust of colleagues.

Depending on their roles and what their jurisdiction looks like, I always say, "Take three to six months to go out into the field and listen to what's going on. Find out what gripes people have, where they see their opportunities, what are they struggling with from a corporate-management perspective, where they need more invested capital, and what their big issues are. I want them to understand what's happening in each unit. I want the new leaders to travel around, 'press the flesh,' and listen to people. I want them to spend a lot more time listening than dictating, deciding, telling people what to do or even giving advice." This can be very hard for people, but those who are able to make it work do very well at NFP.

Then, I say, "Come back and talk to me about it. Let's walk through it. Let's talk about what people are saying." We have six thousand employees, it's impossible to connect with everyone when you're the CEO. Plus, everybody tends to tell you good things; you don't hear about problems much. As the CEO, it's easy to move into sort of a weird place where you get a little isolated from the information in the field because people are reluctant to tell you the less positive parts of the truth. They're reluctant to give you the bad side of what's going on.

Once we discuss what's happening, then I ask the new leaders to go back and provide people in the field with their thoughts and ideas about what we should do to improve things. I want to hear how they envision that we can bring our operation up to the next level. I want them to collaborate with our employees, to win their trust. I want everyone to roll up their sleeves together to move forward.

TRADE EGO FOR TRANSPARENCY

Ego blinds a lot of leaders. Instead of listening, they dictate what people should do so they can demonstrate the extent of their authority. I don't think that's what people want. Employees want leaders who are good listeners, are willing to work with them, ask questions that reflect genuine interest and care, and are sympathetic to their struggles. They want leaders who want to hear their ideas so they can help them make good decisions. When you do that over and over and over again, people trust you.

I also think leaders need to be painfully honest when you have bad news for people. If you sugarcoat things or if you're not transparent about what probable outcomes will be, everybody remembers it. If you want to be a leader for the long haul, people need to know that you're a stand-up person. They want to know that you will always be straight with them. Even if the message is, "We're closing a division" or "We need to terminate people," they need to know you're going to do it with respect and dignity. You're going to treat people like professionals and do your best to help them through it.

"DULL YOUR SHARP ELBOWS" ONCE YOU RISE TO A LEADERSHIP POSITION

I always say, "Leaders need to dull their sharp elbows." This means that early in your career, you need sharp elbows to move up the ranks in your organization. That means working harder than everyone else to prove you can tackle big projects, take on a lot of work, and jump from project to project. You're self-focused on the advancement of your career, which is fine to a certain extent as you're starting to make your way in the business world. However, you will never become a leader if you don't evolve.

If you continue to be all in it just for yourself, people won't follow you. New leaders need to make a smooth transition to that self-promoting phase to one in which they leverage their own experience and success to help others develop and grow. Once you become a leader, dull those sharp elbows. Find the joy in seeing other people succeed and seek out opportunities to help them along. Become a leader who is authentically celebrating other peoples' successes and keeping their best interests in mind. The whole notion of servant leadership is to lead others to excel and succeed. Selfless leaders motivate people to follow their lead.

PRESSURE-TEST YOUR OPERATION WHEN ALL IS GOING WELL

Leaders certainly spend a lot of time analyzing their operations when things aren't going well. But we need to be just as diligent when things *are* going well. Two or three times a year, I tell my senior executives, "Let's spend time identifying the car that could run that red light and smash into us. Let's try to anticipate any issues before they come at us."

Pressure-testing is a common exercise in the corporate world. But it's usually done when things are falling apart so you have some insight on what the issues are. It's a lot harder when you feel like nothing can stop your progress. It requires creativity and an ability to see several moves ahead. For example, we will discuss what could happen if interest rates move in the wrong direction, or what might happen if regulatory changes emerge that impact our business. What are the emerging technologies that could alter the way business in insurance is conducted? What actions will we take if certain things happen in our wealth management business? These of course are just a few of the many possible issues a business like NFP faces, not to mention now having to model the potential impact of a global pandemic.

In all those areas, we kind of run drills around the collateral effects of these developments and the steps we would take to respond to potential crises. This allows us to be prepared for the downside. It also keeps us humble because it acknowledges that no matter how good things are today, it can all change tomorrow.

New leaders typically don't think this way. It takes experience in dealing with catastrophic events—such as the recession in 2008–09—to be able to anticipate threats and plan responses to them. I think the most important thing that younger people who are running businesses for the first time and assuming positions of leadership can do is to assess potential crises that could undermine your success. Think about the worst case scenario on a regular cycle. Discuss with your team how you would respond to the different components of such a threat. And develop the controls or strategies that can mitigate the risk and protect the enterprise from catastrophe.

SOMETIMES YOU DON'T SEE IT COMING

One challenge most companies never anticipated was the emergence of COVID-19. Everyone was reactive, with varying results. NFP didn't have a plan in place to respond to a global pandemic, but our people-first culture and client focus helped us quickly put one in motion. First, we defined our priorities—employee safety, business continuity, and client support—and then made sure that everything we did from there aligned with one or more of them.

We transitioned ninety-eight percent of our employees to work from home in a very short period of time, established a structure for creating and distributing content to address the flood of client questions, and provided resources to employees facing a variety of new challenges (caregiving, mental and physical health, engagement, and productivity among others). And we increased employee and client communications to create a channel for assessing how they were doing and identifying ways we could help.

There was also an opportunity to accelerate things that we were planning to do but just hadn't had a chance to address yet. We asked employees to step up to lead, including the formation of our Coronavirus Critical Response Team (CCRT), which included five NFP employees from different disciplines including operations, legal, HR, and marketing/communications. We also accelerated the collaboration of our sales, marketing, and sales enablement teams to ensure we were continuing to create new opportunities while clients and prospects were working from home.

When we think about what contributed to our ability to endure the crisis and position the company to thrive post-COVID-19, it comes down to several factors.

- We established a clear set of priorities from the outset and had the discipline to let those priorities guide our actions. This structure provides clarity and consistency that prevents panic and irrational responses.
- We acted thoughtfully and decisively, listening and learning along the way. Waiting for certainty isn't an option, which makes informed courage a necessity.
- Our willingness to invest in new communication platforms, benefit programs, and talent created advantages that we never could have predicted. We didn't make these investments thinking how well they would perform in a global pandemic but they all proved to be outstanding resources particularly in this environment.
- Perhaps most importantly, we reconfirmed that our employees are the heart and soul of everything we do. Putting people first is always the right thing to do.

BUILD CORE COMPETENCIES AROUND EMERGING TECHNOLOGIES

Technology is incredibly important in scaling any business. My advice to new leaders is to develop core competencies around emerging technologies that can benefit your business. Develop a social network associated with the folks who are advancing these technologies to ensure that you're seeing them and that you're constantly in a position to evaluate their potential impact to your business.

We have a team of individuals who comprise our innovation lab. The team leverages the expertise of our subject-matter experts across our entire business to help us evaluate emerging technology opportunities both for the benefits they may have for our clients and as potential investments. The outcome may be a licensing relationship with a company that can help address the problems our employer clients face or we may make an investment in the company through our venture fund. Sometimes we do both.

On the investment side, we look for problem solvers who can benefit from our capital, market expertise and distribution capabilities. If there is an opportunity to have an impact and we believe in the return potential, we invest. The collaboration with start-ups that are so focused on creating tools that remove barriers for growth is an exciting part of our business. And it ties directly to our focus on clients and fostering a collaborative culture.

BE RESILIENT

In 2019, my wife and I completed the Three Peaks Challenge, climbing each of the highest peaks in England, Scotland, and Wales in twenty-four hours. It was one of the more difficult physical things I've done in my life but it was incredibly gratifying. We did it with about twenty people from our U.K. office to raise money for a wonderful U.K.-based charity called the Teenage Cancer Trust.

During that 24-hour period, there were moments when I thought this might not be for me. I trained in advance, but was still feeling the pain. I could have easily given up, but it was important to me, my wife, and the others in the group that I finish. And I did.

It was an example of resilience, a critical combination of who we are and what we've learned along the way. I see resilience in both personal and professional endeavors. People who are highly goal-oriented relentlessly push themselves to finish goals they set. Others face devastating personal circumstances, but somehow find a way to overcome them and thrive. Resilience removes the obstacles that prevent you—and oftentimes those around you—from growing and succeeding.

That's why leaders must be resilient. They can't give up; they have to lead by example when things don't work out. And they have to embrace that failure often clears the path to success. Adversity gives us perspective, it informs future decisions and choices, and makes the successes that much sweeter. Leaders who don't know how to pick themselves up after being knocked down won't be leaders for long.

During the financial crisis, with our stock below $1 a share, it was easy to focus on the perceived loss of value. People were telling us that our company was on the verge of failure and that we were delusional for not accepting that. We chose to focus on painting a picture of a brighter future and then drove full steam ahead toward making that vision a reality. That's resilience.

CULTURE, CARING, COLLABORATION—PEOPLEFIRST

Last, and most importantly, prioritizing your employees and putting them first creates a work environment that is conducive to attracting top talent and outperforming our peers. Driving a culture where employees care for one another and celebrate each other's success not only makes for a great place to want to go each and every day but also has resulted in NFP being recognized among the best places to work for the past four years. It's not only good for business—it's just the right thing to do.

ABOUT DOUG HAMMOND

Doug is the Chairman and Chief Executive Officer of NFP, a leading insurance broker and consultant that provides property and casualty, corporate benefits, retirement and individual solutions.

Since joining NFP in 1999, Doug has held multiple leadership roles, including President, Chief Operating Officer, General Counsel and Head of Strategy. In 2013, Doug led NFP's go-private transaction with Madison Dearborn Partners (MDP), LLC, a leading private equity firm. Doug subsequently led two recapitalizations of NFP, in 2017 and 2019, creating significant opportunities for future growth.

Under his leadership, NFP's revenue has grown to $1.6 billion and received recognition from Business Insurance as the fifth largest global benefits broker by revenue and the sixth largest U.S.-based privately owned broker. The company is also ranked as the tenth largest property and casualty agency by Insurance Journal, and the twelfth largest global insurance broker by Best's Review.

In 2017, NFP launched NFP Ventures, the company's early-stage investment arm. NFP Ventures identifies companies within healthcare tech, fintech, and HR tech that are addressing problems faced by NFP clients. NFP collaborates with clients to better understand their most significant challenges and then works with companies focused on developing innovative solutions, providing funding, expertise, and distribution that advances their progress. This supports a culture of thinking about emerging trends in the context of NFP's business, embracing new technologies, and staying focused on the dynamic needs of colleagues, clients, and communities.

With more than 5,800 team members globally, Doug is especially proud that NFP has been recognized by Business Insurance as one of the best places to work in insurance for three consecutive years (NFP ranked fifth overall in 2020). Doug advances initiatives that expand NFP's capabilities and underscore the company's strong personal commitment to its clients and employees, including active support of inclusion efforts that elevate diversity in all its forms.

In addition to his role at NFP, Doug serves a variety of organizations whose activities align with the business and his focus on community impact. He is a member of the Financial Services Advisory Board of MDP and he serves on the Board of Trustees at Northwell Health, connecting NFP's leadership in employee benefits and pharmaceutical consulting with a health system committed to raising the standard of healthcare for all. In addition, Doug is a member of the Board of Trustees at Fairfield University and a Director on the Nassau County Police Department Foundation Board. He is also a Trustee of the Committee for Economic Development of The Conference Board (CED), a nonprofit, nonpartisan public policy organization working to advance reasoned solutions from business in some of the nation's most critical public policy issues. In addition, Doug co-authored Reinsurance Law, a leading subscription treatise on reinsurance practice and legal trends.

Doug received his bachelor's degree from Fairfield University and law degree from St. John's University School of Law. He lives in Cold Spring Harbor, NY, with his wife Trish. Trish and Doug are the proud parents of four children–John, Will, Joe, and Ava.

C-SUITE PERSPECTIVE: FAROOQ KATHWARI

© M. Kathwari

M. Farooq Kathwari
Chairman, President, and CEO
Ethan Allen Interiors, Inc.

As the chairman and CEO of Ethan Allen since 1988 and the president since 1985, I have had the opportunity, and the pleasure of, leading a well-respected brand for many years. I believe my leadership skills emerged early in life.

EARLY CHALLENGES SHAPE OUR CHARACTER

I grew up in the part of Kashmir that was administered by India. When I was just a little over four years old, my father went on a business trip to the other side, which was administered by Pakistan. He was not able to come back. At that time, everyone believed that the Kashmir conflict would be resolved within a year or so.

The Prime Minister of Pakistan asked my father to become one of the leaders of the Pakistan-administered part of Kashmir called Azad Kashmir. And he did. That decision had repercussions on our family on the other side of the border.

My father and his father decided that my mother and three of us would join our father and we crossed over. I had an older brother and sister ages nine and ten and they stayed with our grandfather in Srinagar. Instead of being on the other side for one year, we ended up living there for ten years. We were declared refugees because we had left everything back home. My father worked in Muzaffarabad, which is the capital and largest city in the Pakistan-administered Azad Kashmir.

The government gave us a house at an elevation of 8,000 feet in Murree, a beautiful place. I grew up in the mountains. I learned to take care of myself, and I learned to ride a horse bareback when I was only six or seven years old. I lived a tough life, but it was a good life.

After ten years, when I was fifteen, we were allowed to go back to the main part of Kashmir, which was Indian administered. Immediately, I got involved with sports, which is what I was doing on the other side as well and became captain of the cricket team. There were a lot of political issues at that time. Once I got to college, I became involved in some issues of student leadership.

But many people helped me, and by a miracle, I ended up in New York at age twenty.

COLLEGE GIVES US VALUABLE LIFE EXPERIENCE

When I was growing up, getting a college education was considered an essential step toward success. But today, many entrepreneurs are achieving success without getting a college education first. We learn from books in college but going through college is a valuable education in life—we learn how to listen to professors and how to interact, work with, and live with people.

Today, people tend to communicate less than we did in the past. Certainly, technology has played a role in that shift. Although there are many ways to learn besides going to college, I still believe that the experience of learning with people and learning from your elders is very important. Social interaction is an important part of the college experience.

Because knowledge is so easily accessible today, many young people think a college education is optional. But I encourage everyone to take the opportunity to benefit from the overall life experience a college education offers.

LEADERSHIP LESSONS FROM CRICKET

Throughout my lifetime, I have developed more than four hundred business teams. The Sports has had a major influence on the way I conduct myself. I believe that experience has also contributed to the way Ethan Allen has grown in the past thirty years.

I spent most of my time as an undergraduate in Kashmir and was captain of my university's cricket team. When I came to America and began attending NYU, I was the captain of the NYU cricket team as well. As the captain, my mantra was, "If you are not playing, you are practicing."

I brought those lessons with me into my career; there are many parallels between leading a cricket team and leading a business. At Ethan Allen, most of our associates understand the principle of cricket, which is that the captain plays with the team, strategizes with the team, leads the team, and cheers the team on. Even though Ethan Allen is a public company, I have always abided by that principle.

ATTITUDE IS THE KEY TO EMBRACING DIFFERENT CULTURES

It was a unique situation in Kashmir. Kashmiri Muslims did not play cricket; they played soccer. But the Kashmiri Hindus did play cricket, and a small minority played field hockey. I was among the first

Kashmiri Muslims to play cricket, and I was the first Kashmiri Muslim to become a captain of a cricket team there.

Yet I never saw people as being different. I saw everyone as people, no different than me. I think a person's ability to embrace different cultures is an individual perspective developed by the way he or she grows up.

In my 2019 memoir, *Trailblazer*, I share that when I came to America and went to a subway station in New York City, I was worried about being able to breathe. I had never been in a subway before. But I looked around and saw that everyone was comfortable there. I thought, "These folks are no different than me." The way we react to people and situations has to do with our own personal attitude.

I don't see people as being different from me, and I don't perceive that people see me as being different from them. I have traveled the world and have spent time in Italy, China, Korea, and Portugal. I have always enjoyed the people, and that is probably because of the respect I have for them. The key to appreciating other people and cultures is simply to adopt the attitude that everyone is important, and everyone has unique talents.

TAKE ADVANTAGE OF TECHNOLOGY, BUT ALWAYS PUT PEOPLE FIRST

Ethan Allen has been in business since 1932 and is a vertically integrated company. We begin with a concept of design and still make seventy-five percent of our products in North America, in our own workshops. We run a retail network that has 1,500 interior designers and other associates. We run marketing and logistics. I have been associated with team leaders at all different levels of the company, from design to manufacturing to logistics to technology.

Today, technology is tremendously important in all areas of our enterprise and thinking. We have to be very much aware of, and up to date on, what is taking place in technology.

Technology is tremendously important in everything we do, including manufacturing, logistics, marketing, and finance. Because of the impact technology has had on society and business, change happens faster than ever. Ten or fifteen years ago, we made smaller changes in our products. In fact, when I became president of Ethan Allen in 1985, the company had not changed the design of its products for fifty years.

But today, change is rapid. Every two or three years, we have to really think about our products and what consumers want. This means that the new breed of leadership today has to be tremendously informed and knowledgeable about technology.

What has *not* changed is the way we conduct our associations with our internal and external associates and partners. We believe we must show respect while being disciplined in the way we conduct our business. That will never change.

As leaders, we have to motivate people and treat them with dignity. In our fast-paced world, those important truths are often given less importance than they should have. On one hand, technology has brought us a lot of great things, but on the other hand, it has also removed personal relationships that we all need. We must embrace and leverage technology, but not at the expense of putting people first.

CONSTANTLY REINVENT YOUR BUSINESS, BUT STAY FOCUSED

I have the privilege of being one of the longest serving CEOs of a public company in America. So, although I started my career in a traditional leadership environment, I recognized early on that continuous reinvention is critical. We are always in the process of reinvention. We want to make sure our offerings are relevant to customers.

Maintaining a manufacturing enterprise in the United States is not easy. It requires some tough decisions. Thirty years back, we had almost thirty manufacturing plants. When manufacturing started going offshore, we knew we would not be competitive if we kept our plants in America, so we had to make some tough decisions. We consolidated our plants, and today we have nine manufacturing operations. Two of them are in Mexico, one is in Honduras, and six are in the United States. These nine plants are now producing at least 400 percent more than what our thirty plants were producing.

Often, it is tempting for leaders to expand their enterprises and get involved with businesses that are unrelated to their original ventures. I believe that can be a difficult strategy to do well. I believe in running one enterprise well, with complete focus. I don't want to be distracted by trying to buy other companies and go into other types of business. When I was leading cricket teams, my philosophy was, "I'm going to run just one team." My philosophy in business is the same. It hasn't been easy, but we've been fortunate that we have thrived using that approach.

I've had the opportunity of taking this company through the process of becoming a public company, taking it private in a management buyout and then taking it public again. The company has endured ups and downs for almost ninety years, and it has been profitable every year.

RESPOND TO DISRUPTIONS BY DIFFERENTIATING YOUR BUSINESS

Many disruptions are taking place in the retail industry. The changes in distribution and fierce competition from the Amazons of the world have put many major brands in our industry out of business. And many others that are still operating are facing great challenges. We've all been impacted by the change that is taking place.

The key to surviving, and thriving, in this environment is to ask yourself, "How can we take advantage of this change?" For us, that has meant a great focus on combining technology with personal service. That is tremendously important today. We have figured out how to harness technology to increase production significantly.

Today, Ethan Allen has about 1,500 interior designers. Back when we did much less business, we had 3,000. But technology has made it easier for our designers to work with clients. We're providing them with 3D imaging and virtual reality, and 600 of them are chatting with customers online.

The area where our differentiation is, and where I believe we have great opportunity is, providing great personal service to customers. Our business requires that, but not every business or individual does. Today, many people are happy to buy their furniture from Amazon, Wayfair, and other online retailers, with no personal interaction.

But I see a shift taking place. Many customers want to go back to the way we did things in the past. They want to interact with retailers in person and enjoy a high level of personalized service. Customers no longer tolerate mediocre service; it has to be excellent to win their business. That's why we always focus on hiring and developing exceptional associates.

Recently, we had 500 of our associates come to our Danbury headquarters for our annual convention, and we recognized about 250 of our top associates for their performance. I believe this focus will always give us a competitive advantage. Many enterprises are caught in the middle—they don't provide great service, and they have a tough time competing on technology.

BE PASSIONATE ABOUT WHAT YOU DO

My advice to anyone who aspires to be a leader is to *do everything with passion.* Try to do your work in the best possible way. Whatever you are doing, give it your best effort. I've always felt that, even if I am cutting my grass, I want to be the best grass cutter. We own a farm upstate, and when I'm working at the farm, I want to be the best possible farmer.

Approach everything you do with a tremendous amount of passion. Do not wait for somebody else to recognize you or give you different opportunities. Initiate it yourself. When you are passionate for your own sake, you will progress to the next level, and people will accept and respect you. If you wait for someone else to lead you upward, that time may never come.

GIVE BACK

I think it's tremendously important for leaders to give back. Give back, not because you are trying to gain something out of it, but because it's the right thing to do. Giving helps others, and it also helps us.

When I published my book in 2019, I had a fireside chat with my good friend, Jeff Sonnenfeld, as part of a three-day convention. Jeff is the Senior Associate Dean for Leadership Programs at Yale University's School of Management, and he is the Lester Crown Professor in the Practice of Management. He's also the founder, president, and CEO of the Yale Chief Executive Leadership Institute—the world's first CEO College.

About five hundred people sat in on our talk. One of the topics we discussed was that a critical element of effective leadership is caring for others, showing them empathy, and giving what we can to help others. After our talk, we conducted a survey of the people who attended. By far, the attendees said the part of our talk they got the most out of was the concept of leaders caring for others and showing them empathy.

Caring for others is critical for all of us as human beings, not just for leaders. If you want to build a great team, it's hard to do that without showing empathy for your team members and customers.

THE TEN LEADERSHIP PRINCIPLES THAT GUIDE ME

I think it is important for leaders to identify, communicate, and lead by certain principles that govern the way they operate. About thirty years back, I established my own ten leadership principles. They have guided my team and me and have been tremendously important.

1. **Be self-confident.** I believe that some leaders exhibit an authoritarian leadership style because they are insecure. But those with self-confidence are able to empower others. Self-confidence is a tremendously important leadership trait.

2. **Work hard.** Leaders have to work hard. It doesn't matter what time period we're talking about.

3. **Strive for excellence and innovation.** Leaders have to constantly look for innovations that will help them and their organizations in all aspects.

4. **Be accessible.** This means being open, supportive, and willing to recognize other people's contributions. It's about listening with open ears and an open mind.

5. **Maintain a customer focus.** Regardless of how large your enterprises are, customer focus is critical.

6. **Prioritize.** It is a leader's responsibility to prioritize action because not everything is equally critical. When I arrive to our office in Connecticut every day, I take a route called 684. It takes almost an hour for me to drive here. I think a lot during that drive. And almost every day, I ask myself, "What's the most important thing we need to do today and this week?" I write those priorities down on a notepad. It doesn't take much time to do important step, but I'm amazed at the number of people who don't do it. Taking a few minutes to prioritize your work for the day and week can save you a lot of time in the end.

7. **Lead by example.** Leaders set the standard for everyone else to follow. We must be cognizant of how our actions and words affect those around us.

8. **Embrace change.** Change means opportunity, and we can't be afraid of it.

9. **Act with speed.** I like to use the U.S. Marine Corps as an example. They operate by what's called "the 70 percent solution." The principle is that, whether on the battleground or in business, we

will never have all the information we need to make a wise decision, especially when action must be taken immediately. We don't have the luxury of waiting until we're one hundred percent ready. So, the Marines act when they believe they have about seventy percent of the facts they need to take decisive action. That speed in making decisions, especially under duress, is critical for leaders.

10. **Impart justice.** This is a concept that people generally don't use in business, but I think it matters profoundly. At Ethan Allen, we have tried to apply it in many areas of our business. We have an excellent record of social responsibility in the way we conduct our business.

All ten of these principles are tremendously important in terms of managing an enterprise. As leaders in a changing world, we are faced with many challenges, including fierce competition, demanding customers, economic uncertainty, and ensuring that our organizations are committed to D&I. These principles have helped my team and me navigate and overcome those challenges.

ABOUT M. FAROOQ KATHWARI

Farooq Kathwari is the chairman, president, and CEO of Ethan Allen Interiors Inc. He has been president of the company since 1985 and chairman and CEO since 1988.

Mr. Kathwari serves in numerous capacities at several nonprofit organizations. He is a member of the Board of Overseers of the International Rescue Committee, a member of the advisory board of the Center for Strategic and International Studies, a member of the Council on Foreign Relations, chairman emeritus of Refugees International, an advisory member of the New York Stock Exchange, former chairman of the National Retail Federation, director emeritus and former chairman and president of the American Home Furnishings Alliance, a director of the Institute for the Study of Diplomacy at Georgetown University, co-chairman of the Muslim–Jewish Advisory Council, and a member of the International Advisory Council of the United States Institute of Peace.

Mr. Kathwari also serves on the boards of the Western Connecticut State University Foundation, The Hebrew Home at Riverdale, and ArtsWestchester.

He is the founder of the Kashmir Study Group. From 2010 to 2014, he was a member of the President's Advisory Commission on Asian Americans and Pacific Islanders.

Recently, Mr. Kathwari was tapped to join the bipartisan, congressionally mandated United States Institute of Peace Task Force on Extremism in Fragile States, co-chaired by Governor Tom Kean and Representative Lee Hamilton, who formerly led the 9/11 Commission.

Among his many recognitions, Mr. Kathwari is a recipient of the 2018 Ellis Island Medal of Honor and has been inducted into the American Furniture Hall of Fame. He has been recognized as an Outstanding American by Choice by the U.S. government. He received the Yale School of Management's Chief Executive Leadership Institute Lifetime of Leadership Award, the New American Dream Foundation's

Lifetime Achievement Award, the Connecticut Institute for Refugees and Immigrants Legacy Award, the Eleanor Roosevelt Val–Kill Medal; the National Human Relations Award from the American Jewish Committee, the National Retail Federation Gold Medal, the International First Freedom Award from the Council for America's First Freedom, Ernst & Young's Entrepreneur of the Year Award, the Anti-Defamation League's Humanitarian Award, the City of Hope's International Home Furnishings Industry Spirit of Life® Award, and the Entrepreneurial Excellence Award from the National Association of Asian MBAs. *Worth* magazine recognized him as one of the 50 Best CEOs in the United States.

Mr. Kathwari is the author of *Trailblazer: From the Mountains of Kashmir to the Summit of Global Business and Beyond*, a memoir he published in September 2019. The book focuses on Mr. Kathwari's journey from Kashmir to America, his association with Ethan Allen, and his involvement with conflict resolution and humanitarian causes.

Mr. Kathwari holds BA degrees in English literature and political science from Kashmir University, Srinagar, and an MBA in International Marketing from NYU. He is also the recipient of three honorary doctorate degrees. For more information, visit farooqkathwari.com.

C-SUITE PERSPECTIVE: EILEEN MCDONNELL

© E. McDonnell

Eileen McDonnell
Chairman and CEO
Penn Mutual

Everyone defines leadership differently. Some people think it's about creating a vision, for example. For me, leadership is inspiring others to strive to be more than they ever thought they could be.

I consider my leadership style to be collaborative, authentic, transparent, and open. I was using that leadership style long before it was in vogue. I think we see more of that today than we did fifteen to twenty years ago. I have always recognized the value of individuals who have been around me and known that they could complement my strengths and fill my gaps. There are individuals who can make me better, and hopefully, in some way, I can make them better along the way.

For more than a decade, I have been looking at the insurance and financial services industry business model with a skeptical eye. I have led our team of financial professionals through some systemic challenges. One is that corporations often lump people into categories, or "buckets," such as career agent versus independent agent, instead of viewing each advisor as an individual with unique talents.

UPGRADE TRADITIONAL MODELS THAT AREN'T WORKING

If you're a visionary, you see opportunities for improvement long before people can.

When I arrived at Penn Mutual in 2008, I had already been in the industry for twenty years. I introduced a concept here called *channel fluidity*. I recognized that the most important thing any leader or organization can provide a financial professional is an environment in which they can be most productive. That is different for each person.

With channel fluidity as the goal, we began coaching life insurance professionals using advanced marketing concepts to accelerate the growth of their practices and enable them to diversify into new markets and either expand or transition their businesses. We encourage independent financial professionals to move within the company's distribution channels to facilitate the growth of their businesses.

This concept has enabled Penn Mutual's distribution partners to leverage the best aspects of both their independent and career channels so they can grow their businesses and increase life insurance sales revenue. It has led to a positive, permanent culture change. Penn Mutual has seen a marked reduction in channel conflict, improved succession-planning outcomes, and significantly increased life insurance sales revenue.

We've seen professionals who started out in a career shop and had the benefit of working under a great leader, but then the leadership changed, and the person did not thrive under the new leadership. Instead of losing their experience and talent to another company, this concept gives us the flexibility to keep them on board.

Companies often let those individuals walk away after making a huge investment in training and developing them. For example, a company I worked for had both a career channel and an independent channel, but they wouldn't let advisors cross those lines. That has been commonplace in the industry. Companies that did allow some flexibility would make advisors wait for a year or two between the time they worked in an agency until they could go to the independent side. Advisors would walk away, become independent representatives somewhere else, or find new career "homes" and, in most cases, never come back to their original company.

The economics weren't working, either. I started having our organization look through the lens of the financial professionals and walking in their shoes. I asked our leadership team to consider how we could help them be most productive and put them into the environment in which they could best succeed. Whether it is a career system, an independent system, a strategic alliance, or a producer group—whatever you want to call it—I want to make sure we facilitate advisors to finding the right homes. Our hope is that, as a reward for doing that, those advisors will be endeared to us and want to continue to do business under whatever business model they prefer.

This is a disruptive breakthrough that has been positive for the industry.

GOOD RIDDANCE TO THE "COMMAND AND CONTROL" LEADERSHIP STYLE

The command-and-control style of leadership of decades past doesn't work anymore. That approach so says, "I want to do this. So, let's do it now." But leaders can only get performance out of people for so long with that approach. Our world has changed dramatically in the past decade, and it's changing faster and faster. As a result, we are seeing an unprecedented flexibility around work styles. Today, leaders are more effective when we bring people along and include them in the process.

Sometimes the timeline for achieving success takes much longer than we'd like. It can be frustrating when we have to abide by other people's timelines and get them to absorb what we're seeing. This is especially true for visionary leaders who can see their desired outcomes so clearly, but others cannot.

I don't believe that past performance is indicative of future success anymore. Someone who didn't thrive in the past could have been stifled by ineffective leadership or an environment that wasn't open to the value they brought to the organization. We have to meet our team members where they are and allow them to work in the environment that enables them to thrive. That's great for financial professionals, and it's great for the company.

TREAT CUSTOMERS WITH RESPECT—WHETHER THEY'RE CUSTOMERS OR TEAM MEMBERS

Penn Mutual does not do direct-to-consumer business; our financial professionals are our customers. We knew it was important to focus on getting advisors into the right environment, giving them the right training, helping them be productive, and treating them with respect.

It sounds simple, but many of our competitor companies were viewing advisors almost like interchangeable parts. Ironically, for a relationship business, some companies walked away from having strong relationships and knowing that people want to do business with people they like.

Also, as data and data science become more advanced, I see more and more leaders who are becoming dependent on data-driven decisions. Effective leaders recognize both left-brain (analytical) and right-brain (creative) skills. We are all humans, and we all have basic human emotions. It concerns me that many leaders are letting technology override the human element of our business.

It was easy for advisors to leave that approach behind. We became known as the home of financial professionals who were looking for a place where they could be respected for the work they did with their clients, valued as individuals, and appreciated for the contributions they are making to Penn Mutual.

LET PEOPLE KNOW WHAT WILL HELP YOU SUCCEED

I can attribute my success, in part, to my willingness to ask for help. Along the way, I have asked individuals to help me understand either things I didn't know about the roles I was in or the business around me. People were very generous to share their knowledge with me.

I think most men and women are afraid to ask for help because they think it's a sign of weakness. I've seen that this is particularly true for women. When I was given the opportunity to interview with Penn Mutual for the role of Chief Marketing Officer, I interviewed with the board of directors and with the CEO. I was very clear with them that I had experienced a great career, had been president of New England Financial and stepped away, adopted my daughter, created a consultancy, and taught at The American College. If they were not going to provide a flexible enough workplace for me to be able to raise my daughter, whom I had gone halfway around the world to adopt in my mid-forties, then I was not interested in a job here.

Some people have asked me, "How were you brave enough to say that?" I had to be candid because I knew I could not be successful as an executive or feel confident that I was doing my role as a good mom if I had not laid that out on the table.

During the interview, I said, "I want to be able to go to my daughter's kindergarten class and be a mystery reader like every other parent. I don't want to be the parent who can't go because I'm an executive or CEO of a company."

The board and the CEO were fine with that. But I had to speak up about it. There was a chance it wouldn't work out for me. They could have said, "Sorry. We're not looking for that."

We have to ask for those things. That goes for pay as well. To ensure pay equity, you have to know what you're worth in the marketplace. People need to be aware of what you need, as an individual, to be as successful as possible.

WORK TO ACHIEVE D&I

I think our society still places a lot of parenting responsibilities into the hands of women, but we're seeing a shift toward more parity in the younger generations. Although we're not at 50/50 yet, more men are picking up nontraditional duties at home, which is nice to see for everybody involved.

Still, though, women often have to talk about things that men don't. We have worked hard to create a flexible environment here. We allow flexibility for our financial professionals and staff so they can take care of young children, care for elderly parents, or pursue other activities outside work—whether they're male or female. But outside Penn Mutual, women in particular often have to prioritize what's important to them. They have to set expectations, both at work and at home, about what they're going to be able to do to be successful. I see a shift in this area that's giving both men and women more flexibility to tend to what they need to, without which it is affecting their ability to succeed.

Penn Mutual was only one of seven companies in the Fortune 1000 that has both a female CEO and a female CFO until the CFO's retirement in 2020. This is welcome progress. Decades ago, women in leadership positions felt like they had to be grateful they were given the opportunity. But today, I am seeing more women being promoted into positions of leadership. Working with mentors and sponsors can help women move past traditional barriers to leadership.

We are proud that forty-five percent of the members of our board are females and two are African Americans. As a matter of fact, Penn Mutual has had either a woman or a person of color on our board, uninterrupted since the 1970s. We have a unique situation in that we have always recognized that the contributions of both women and people of color are important to our organization.

I spend a lot of time mentoring women and helping them see and seize opportunities along the way. Recently, I spoke in front of 275 women in Philadelphia at an event that was about how to get to the C-suite. In both small and large forums, I try to help women succeed. I think the most important thing for women—and men—to do is to understand what you really want. Everybody has different aspirations for themselves, and we all view success through different lenses. Being in the C-suite or being the CEO is not for everyone. Know what you truly want—and then go for it!

Millennials tend to have a great grasp of segmenting their lives. I see that generation controlling their destiny at the entry levels of the organization, and they will continue to do so as they move through the ranks of workforce. I think that eventually, most leaders will make D&I a priority. Thanks to the millennials, I think women have gotten a boost in becoming more vocal about what their needs are in the workplace.

I probably sit an enviable position in that we do have a long history of diversity on our board. We seek the most talented individuals at all levels to take our company where we believe needs to go, but ensuring D&I still requires work. It requires constant communication, seeking advice, and encouraging a collaborative work style with both the team I work with day to day and with the board, who is technically my boss.

Our leadership team and the board reach out to each other by, for example, sending each other articles of interest. And we celebrate one another's milestones, whether it's a birthday or the birth of a child or grandchild. I want to nurture relationships so they can continue to grow and evolve, just as I've grown and evolved in my position as CEO.

WALK AWAY FROM YOUR LOSSES

Every leader experiences both successes and disappointments.

When I was president of New England Financial, I really thought I could turn that company around from being a loss leader for MetLife. I put a lot of blood, sweat, and tears into trying to shift the direction of the organization's performance in a very short period of time—less than two years.

But the organization made a decision that made that goal unreachable. That was a learning experience for me. I had to recognize what is humanly possible and what's not. I finally accepted that no matter how much effort I put in, that was not going to be a successful outcome.

In some regards, I was raising my hand and almost putting myself out of work by saying, "This organization isn't capable of delivering on the results and schedule it needs to meet." Sometimes you just have to walk away from your losses. Even if you want to see something successful, sometimes it just doesn't make good business sense to pursue it.

EMULATE THE WORLD'S INNOVATIONS IN YOUR OWN COMPANY

I watch change in the world around me that has nothing to do with my business. For example, people used to buy tickets for movies and performances at the box-office window, but now we do that online, to a large extent. I am an Amazon Prime member, and I pay attention to all the different experiences as a general consumer and a participant in today's world. I try to discover how I can bring some of those innovations into this company to impact the business I'm leading. I ask myself, "How could we innovate to make our business more relevant in a world that has changed so dramatically?"

It takes discipline to wake up every day and look at what we're doing. It starts with looking at your agenda or schedule for the day and asking, "Is this really the best use of my time? Am I focusing on the things that will impact us tomorrow?" I pull in what I see around me. I talk to people from the outside. One of the things I pride myself in doing is having some confidants who have rather extreme views, compared to mine. Spending time understanding their views helps me shape and reshape my views.

This is true not just of our colleagues, but of our children as well. I think we can learn as much from our kids as they learn from us. The awesome responsibility of motherhood—preparing another human being to be successful in the world—has taught me a lot of great skills, including patience.

LEADING DURING THE PANDEMIC

The pandemic presented us with a combination of completely new challenges and some that were similar to obstacles we've overcome in our 174-year history. As always, because our primary focus is on the long-term needs of our policyholders, our diversified investment strategies and disciplined financial management served us well. Because of our investment in technology and focus on scenario planning, we were already equipped to move to a complete remote work environment within a matter of days.

Although we've always prioritized the safety, health, and well-being of our employees, the pandemic created completely new challenges in some regards. To help guide us, we stayed true to our culture of care, respect, and belonging during this time. We provided flexibility and offered a full range of health and wellness resources to our employees and their families to help them manage responsibilities. We communicated regularly and with great transparency to ensure our teams stayed informed and connected. We created opportunities for virtual gatherings and found creative ways to adapt some of our most treasured traditions, including charitable giving, peer-to-peer recognition programs, and fun employee activities to maintain pride, spirit, and engagement.

As this book goes to print, we're more than a year into working remotely, and I'm proud to say we've delivered seamless service to our financial professionals and their clients. We've also provided our financial professionals with tools, resources, and programs to help them adapt to and succeed in a virtual sales and service environment. Because our business is relationship-based, it's been gratifying to see so many people rely on us during this time. The trust and credibility we earned well before the pandemic has only deepened during this time.

ABOUT EILEEN C. MCDONNELL

Eileen C. McDonnell has been chairman and chief executive officer of Penn Mutual since July 2013. She was appointed CEO in 2011 and president in 2010, after serving as chief marketing officer since 2008.

Before joining Penn Mutual, she was president of New England Financial, a wholly owned subsidiary of MetLife, and senior vice president of the Guardian Life Insurance Company. Ms. McDonnell is a former member of the Master of Science in Management faculty at The American College in Bryn Mawr, Pennsylvania, where she held the newly endowed chair for Women and Financial Services. She is the author of *Marketing Financial Services to Women.*

Ms. McDonnell serves on the Board of Managers of Janney Montgomery Scott LLC, a wholly owned subsidiary of Penn Mutual. She serves on the board of the Insurance Federation of Pennsylvania and is the Lead Independent Director of the Board of Universal Health Services, Inc. (NYSE: UHS). In 2016, she was named to the Drexel LeBow Center for Corporate Governance Advisory Board.

A graduate of Molloy College in Rockville Centre, New York, Ms. McDonnell majored in mathematics and computer science and received an honorary Doctor of Laws (LLD) degree in 2011. She earned her MBA in finance and investments from Adelphi University in Garden City, New York, and was recognized in 2013 for "Outstanding Service" to the university.

C-SUITE PERSPECTIVE: KATHLEEN MURPHY

© K. Murphy

Kathleen Murphy
President, Personal Investing at Fidelity Investments

The corporate world must embrace the opportunities and challenges of adapting to our quickly changing, digitally enabled world. This has become even more pronounced as a result of the changes brought on by the pandemic to business models, employees' work habits and needs, and new client demands.

The structure of most large corporate organizations worldwide—not just in America—hasn't fundamentally changed since World War II. Most large companies are organized into large functional groupings, even at the business-unit level. They require groups of employees to work across matrices to bring products and solutions to market. While this fundamental structure has served corporations well for decades, it is not built to compete effectively against fast-paced, digitally born competitors. As business leaders, we must ask ourselves, "How can we lead differently and organize our businesses differently to get more value to customers more quickly in the digital economy?"

If your company is not "born digital," the challenge is to become "reborn digitally." To be successful requires a deep cultural shift, a refreshed approach to leadership, and a nimbler organizational structure to enable dedicated and integrated teams of empowered associates to deliver value with much greater speed and an agile mindset. Those large, functional silos with layers of management often impede "speed to value." Stepping back and thinking about a very different organizational structure to compete more effectively with digitally born companies that are organized very differently is an imperative.

Specifically, regarding leadership, I think it's very important to move from a "command and control" type of environment to an empowering environment based on the concept of servant leadership. This involves empowering your people once you establish a clear strategy and specific outcomes to achieve, listening more to their feedback, removing obstacles for them, and creating a digital ecosystem to enhance productivity.

ADJUST AS THE BREADTH OF YOUR LEADERSHIP ROLE EVOLVES

Throughout my career, my leadership style has adjusted as I have learned more, primarily for two reasons. First, there's a natural evolution for leaders to learn as they grow (and make mistakes!) and seek to make themselves more effective. Second, leaders need to continually enhance our leadership based on the emergence of new capabilities, tools, and technologies that can improve a leader's effectiveness and reach.

In the digital world we live in, for example, there are innumerable new ways of helping our associates by investing in new learning capabilities, enhanced communication capabilities, and technologies to improve productivity. This became even more urgent during the global pandemic, which forced most people to work remotely. Those companies and leaders that invested in these capabilities prior to the pandemic were much better positioned to conduct their businesses remotely.

Your leadership style also has to evolve to match the breadth of the job you are in. We see many entrepreneurs, for example, begin their start-ups with a few employees. As some of these companies become successful, they grow to have hundreds or thousands of employees. At that point, their leadership role and style must adjust to these dramatically changed circumstances.

This is similar to what many first-time leaders face as their responsibilities grow. For leaders at all levels, as you move from "doing" to managing increasingly larger groups of people, you have to step back and ask yourself, "How do I add value *now*?" With growth comes even more responsibilities. What level of detail should you focus on? Where should you be diving deep, versus not? Generally speaking, I think good leaders are always curious about how effective they are in supporting their teams during that growth, and they are willing to adapt and always welcome extremely candid feedback.

Each one of us has natural dispositions—specific attributes in our DNA that enable us to excel in certain aspects of leadership. There isn't just one leadership style that works. My advice to young leaders who are beginning their careers is to remember that ***authenticity*** is number one—the most important thing. Second is *self-awareness*—knowing what you are good at and what are your "watch-outs." As you gain more responsibility, be relentless about understanding what the organization needs from you and how effective you are in meeting those needs in a way that is true to who you are and that leverages your natural strengths.

CELEBRATE—AND REWARD—DIVERSITY OF THOUGHT AND INCLUSIVITY

While the dynamics involving D&I in corporations are changing, much more progress is needed. Corporate America has been talking about this for a very long time, but progress has been elusive in some important areas.

As a woman in financial services, I have certainly seen "unconscious bias" in action in a variety of ways over the course of my career. More broadly, the historical lack of diverse perspectives and inclusivity has had a significant impact on the lack of effectiveness of the financial services industry in serving women and people of color as customers.

A critical responsibility I have as a leader is to ensure every person in my organization has the opportunity to truly reach his or her full potential. And I want to make sure we do everything possible to bring the best of our organization to bear for the diverse customers we serve. At its core, that's also how I think about diversity and inclusivity. It's creating an environment in which companies attract strong and diverse talent and enable those team members to bring their full selves to work, grow continually, and achieve their full potential. Leaders need to be held accountable for achieving ongoing progress on both broader diversity and deeper inclusivity in order for the business to achieve its full potential. And efforts to improve both diversity of the employee base at all levels and enhanced inclusivity need to be both actively celebrated and rewarded to reinforce the right behaviors and efforts.

There is a significant opportunity, for example, in the financial services industry to dramatically broaden our customer reach and enhance the effectiveness of the company by broadening the diversity of the associate base and challenging traditional ways of thinking.

One micro-example of one of my efforts was to attract more women advisors in our branches. As we analyzed some of the drivers of attracting female advisors and sought their candid feedback, we challenged the rationale for a range of traditional workplace policies and flexibility that, in general, had been long-entrenched. We tackled these policies head-on and modernized those policies in response to that candid feedback. I am proud to say that since the inception of this effort several years ago, we significantly increased the number of women financial professionals in our branches.

It quickly became clear that the benefit of these changes helped everyone, not just women. Thus, the changes—driven by a goal to broaden our diversity for the benefit of our associates and clients—benefited everyone and allowed us to also provide greater inclusivity.

THE CHALLENGE OF WORK–LIFE BALANCE, PARTICULARLY DURING THE PANDEMIC

With respect to the challenges of work–life balance, my advice pre-pandemic would have been to use ruthless prioritization in order to be successful in managing what's most important to you at different stages of your life. If your work and your family are most important to you, particularly when your children are younger, then you will probably have to delay other priorities until your children get older. The saying that "you can have it all, just not all at the same time" is very true.

Again, the pandemic has surfaced fresh challenges as work and our personal lives have blended together when working from home full time. This has led to increased stress, mental health concerns, and a variety of balance issues.

Studies have shown that this has disproportionately affected certain groups, such as women and people of color. Leaders at all levels need to be hyper-vigilant to the concerns and impact that such a situation has on associates at all levels. The pandemic has also reinforced the proactive need for inclusivity efforts. In a remote environment, for example, there's often more sensitivity from employees about having colleagues see their personal environments. With the increased isolation, there can also be a tendency to work with, seek out, and provide opportunities to people we are comfortable with, which again can leave certain groups such as women and people of color at a disadvantage.

With hybrid work arrangements expected to continue past the pandemic period, this is another critical area that leaders need to be focused on to avoid disenfranchisement of their employees.

SIX LEADERSHIP REMINDERS

Here are six leadership reminders that emerged as lessons for me throughout my career:

1. **Empower others to excel.** When leaders believe they must have all the answers, they tend to go pretty deep into the details. That is not the best use of our time. Effective leadership requires having good judgment about what to handle personally and what to delegate. This requires that we empower those around us to make the best use of their talents … and be relentless about removing any obstacles or friction that diminish empowerment.

2. **Always set a high bar for excellence.** The legendary coach Vince Lombardi once said, "The quality of a person's life is in direct proportion to their commitment to excellence, regardless of their chosen field of endeavor." This is true in all fields. Effective leaders in any organization focus on helping their employees reach their individual and collective full potential and pursuing excellence for their organization overall. Create an environment worthy of your associates' best efforts, and then motivate them to achieve big goals.

3. **Have fun!** Growing a business is hard work for you and everyone around you. Do what you can to inspire and celebrate your team. They're going to feel much more motivated and have a better sense of belonging if there is a common purpose and a sense that "We're in this together." Have some fun along the way.

4. **Focus on what you enjoy, not on your title.** Too often, I see people trying to chase a title instead of focusing on what really gives them fulfillment. If you focus on what fulfills you, including the broader purpose of your business for the benefit of the customers you serve, you will go further than if you're chasing titles.

5. **Show that you care.** People want to know that their leaders truly care about them, that they are listening and acting on their feedback, and that they have empathy for them.

6. **Be authentic.** Again, I believe it is critical for leaders to be authentic and down-to-earth. Be someone people can *look up to* while also being someone they can *relate to.*

ABOUT KATHLEEN MURPHY

As the President, Personal Investing at Fidelity Investments, Kathleen Murphy led a significant expansion of the product, services, and capabilities of Fidelity's retail investing business to a full-service wealth-management and brokerage business in the past decade. In her leadership role, she oversaw a near quadrupling of clients' assets in her business to more than $3.6 trillion.

Ms. Murphy joined Fidelity in 2009 as President of Personal Investing, which provides a full range of investment and financial planning services to millions of individual investors, including wealth management, retirement planning, and brokerage. She also oversaw Fidelity's life insurance and annuities business, its workplace savings business for tax-exempt organizations, all of the firm's brand and advertising programs, its Artificial Intelligence Center of Excellence, and Fidelity's various digital programs.

Prior to joining Fidelity, Ms. Murphy was CEO of ING US Wealth Management, leading the Defined Contribution, Defined Benefit, Retirement Solutions, Annuities, and ING Advisors Network businesses. She began her career with Aetna, spending fifteen years in a variety of legal and government affairs positions, eventually serving as general counsel and chief compliance officer for Aetna Financial Services.

Among her many honors, she was repeatedly named one of the "50 Most Powerful Women in American Business" by *Fortune* magazine, one of the "Wall Street Top 50" and "Business 100" by *Irish America* magazine, and one of the "25 Most Powerful Women in Finance" by *US Banker*.

QUOTES BY TARIQ KHAN

The worst place for Diversity & Inclusion is in your "to do list."

The difference between working for others and entrepreneurship is that working for others guarantees your salary but not your job, entrepreneurship guarantees your job but not your salary.

FINAL THOUGHTS

Every day, you will come across many people and many reasons why you shouldn't be a leader. Ask yourself these questions:

1. Why do I want to be a leader?
2. What impact do I want to make?
3. Do I believe in myself?

You must be uncompromisingly transparent with yourself as to why you really want to become a leader. One of the most important reason many people want to become a leader is to leave a legacy, but they don't acknowledge it. If you have clarity about your answers to these questions, then let your leadership journey roll. If you are committed enough and meant to be a leader, you will become a leader. *Being* a leader is not as difficult as *staying* a leader. Here is my advice once you become a leader:

1. You real crucible starts now; create your leadership strategy.
2. Choose the *right* people, not necessarily the *best* people.
3. Separate yourself from wrong people, no matter how good they are.
4. Set your milestones and monitor them—no compromises.
5. Listen to those who provide constructive feedback, not those who always praise you.

FINAL ADMONISHMENT: TEN DANGERS TO AVOID

Here are some avoidable perilous areas that leaders must avoid. Some of the greatest leaders fall prey to these dangers. You could be at the peak of your career, and they can come from the left field and disrupt your career:

1. Health issues
2. Scandals
3. Choosing the wrong partner(s)
4. Getting involved in controversies
5. Poor branding or a lack of branding
6. Failing to be presentable at all times
7. Influenced by advisors
8. Letting it get to your head
9. Not learning from women around you (for male leaders)
10. Not being crystal clear on your end goal

Let's look at each of these dangers in more detail.

1. HEALTH ISSUES

Health is a key to success, happiness, and a good life. Death is predictable, but health is quite unpredictable. Of course, some fatal diseases are unpredictable and out of control, but many diseases like heart problem, strokes, and diabetes are often the result of an unhealthy lifestyle.

Leaders must stay in good health and stay fit. They should exercise regularly, eat healthy, and get ample sleep (no compromises). Please ensure to incorporate a work–life balance in life. It is a cliché and often misunderstood. I have seen many young leaders say that my work is my passion and I enjoy life the most when I'm at work. While that may be true, but you must divide your time in three buckets:

1. Professional work
2. Time with your family/friends
3. Time with yourself

It is important to understand and categorize the different slots. When you are at work, give all that you have to work. This is a perception that leaders are always at work. No, they are at work when they are at work. While it may be okay to take your family to a company conference but then spending the majority of the time on company agenda and pre-determined excursions with office workers/family cannot be termed as family time. The real family time is uninterrupted; hard but doable. The time with yourself is also an important part of work–life balance. This is the time you spend with yourself doing things that makes you happy.

Many leaders travel alone frequently for work and find themselves at exotic places. They end up spending most of the time at the airport, meetings, and the hotel room. Take some time out and enjoy the place. One day, you don't want to say that I have been to many places, but I have seen so few. The self-time can also be at home watching your favorite show on your tablet, reading your favorite book, or anything else that gives you pleasure.

The whole idea behind work–life balance is to have a happy and healthy life and caring for your loved ones. Don't make the mistake of giving your entire self to your professional life. You may achieve the professional success, but you may not enjoy the benefits for too long. You owe it your family and yourself.

Good health is a luxury, not an entitlement. We only realize this once we lose good health. Enjoy while the supplies last and do your best to protect your health.

2. SCANDALS

Scandals, affairs, and undesirable relationships are a result of poor judgment. History has been a witness to numerous "could have been a great" leaders who capitulated to extramarital affairs, dated their direct reports, accepted free trips from potential vendors, or got too drunk on a night out.

Scandals are cardinal sins for leaders. When in doubt, leave it out.

3. CHOOSING THE WRONG PARTNER(S)

Our family members are given to us; we don't choose them. We choose our friends, life partners, and business partners. Having a wrong partner in life or business can destroy you beyond your imagination, and sometimes beyond repair. At times, they are not bad people; they are just not right for you. Be careful in selecting partners and friends. Right partners and friends are a great asset, and wrong partners and friends are a great liability.

Don't procrastinate disassociating from the wrong partners and friends; it is good for both of you.

4. GETTING INVOLVED IN CONTROVERSIES

Leaders should be bold and take a stand regarding their values and core beliefs; however, there are some no-go areas. At all costs, avoid getting involved in controversies related to incendiary topics such as religion and political positioning. People's opinions on these topics are quite strong and don't change easily. A leader's life is public—even in private. However, don't shy away from taking a stand on what you believe is right. At times, your silence becomes your position, which often can be misrepresented.

Avoid voicing your religious and political opinions. It ain't worth it!

5. POOR BRANDING OR A LACK OF BRANDING

Branding is perception, and perception becomes reality. Recognition and accolades are not official until *others* start talking about your accomplishments. How do other people give you accolades? Branding has been defined as what people say about you when you're not around.

You might worry that your great work is the best kept secret and may never receive proper appreciation. Your recognition should grow organically, but there is a strategy behind that. It usually involves presenting your progress in the right medium at the right time through the right channel.

Avoid talking about your own accomplishments constantly. Make such an impact that others *want* to talk about them.

6. FAILING TO BE PRESENTABLE AT ALL TIMES

Leaders need to look good and presentable. People look up to you, and some idolize you. Leaders need to take care of themselves. Dress well, be groomed, and stay clean. Pay attention to how you appear.

We tend to follow people who look good and tidy. Work on your posture, communication, eye contact, handshake, and interaction with people. Your body language is equally important. After all, you are a leader, and you need to give people many reasons to follow you. Of course, you don't want to put all your focus on your appearance and disappoint on content. Otherwise, you will be known as an "empty suit"—and yes, there are many of those.

Don't worry about things you can't change but make all possible efforts to appear sharp and attractive.

7. INFLUENCED BY ADVISORS

Leaders always attract advisors, some desirable and many undesirables. In all likelihood, you will be surrounded by an army of flatterers and yeasayers. Not all your advisors are bad. It is a leader's job to differentiate between the imbecile, innocuous, and sincere people. Also remember, not all sincere people always give you the right advice. Many leaders tend to discuss their challenges with their family (spouses and kids), they are quite sincere, but their advice, at times, may be emotional and not in your best interests. They are not seeing things from your lens and are not privy to all the information. Thus, their advice is often based on gut feelings and biased.

A good leader will distance herself/himself from undesirable advisors and always listen to close professional confidants who are not afraid to disagree. Also, don't have a blind leap of faith in your domestic partner's gut feelings, even if they have been right in the past. Make decisions based on facts and your insights. Never feel obligated to follow someone's advice because you care for them, and you may hurt them if you don't follow their advice. The well-intended advice is not always germane to your problem. Your right decisions will benefit them as well.

Decisions based on emotions often lead to undesirable results.

8. LETTING IT GET TO YOUR HEAD

It is quite normal to feel proud of your accomplishments; however, at times, the line between feeling proud and feeling arrogant is often crossed. Only the great leaders are able to demonstrate their humility as they grow. Of course, acting as a servant leader is the ideal position but not everyone can carry that well. Only genuine leaders do. How you feel may be different than how you are perceived.

The stature of your leadership is not judged by how you feel but how others see you.

9. NOT LEARNING FROM WOMEN AROUND YOU

Many men think in black and white, and many women think in color. I can't scientifically prove this, but I strongly feel that it is true. I also believe that women are made superior and more gifted in many ways. Many male leaders are binary thinkers and lack the capacity of seeing things from a wider lens. As I am maturing, I am beginning to look at things from a wider perspective. My conversations with my wife made me realize that I have completely missed out on how different woman are in terms of their emotions, approach, and feelings. I still have a lot to learn but I am getting better or so I think.

I have also learned a great deal about the next generation from my daughter Alina and my nieces, Mahnoor and Maheen. These young ladies have taught me more about diversity, gender equity, and inclusiveness than I have learned as a diversity practitioner in decades. I recommend all male leaders pay attention when they talk to other women who provide them independent opinions. Please understand that half of world's population is women. They are your family members, your coworkers, and your customers. You simply can't ignore them.

10. NOT BEING CRYSTAL CLEAR ON YOUR END GOAL

How do you want to be remembered? What are you willing and able to do to make this happen? These are the two basic questions every leader must ask and answer before hanging their shoes. If I want to be remembered as the best basketball player, I should know this immediately that neither do I have the ability nor the willingness to do that at this point in my life. It is a non-starter. Make your ambitious goal that leaves an impact and makes a difference to people other than you. However, you must have the capacity and skills to achieve that goal. Nothing wrong with adding a personal goal to your professional goal.

I have changed my goals or better yet adjusted my goals as per my priorities over the years. You must set your own priorities, not what everyone is doing or what is popular but what is more aligned with your goals.

My professional life is divided into three buckets:

	My time spent today (%)	Goal (my time in 10 years) (%)
Running my business	60	10
Teaching	20	40
Serving non-profit organizations	20	50

I do not plan to wait for the tenth yeat to bring this change, it will happen gradually. All three professional buckets in my life require leadership. The best part of all these leadership verticals is the opportunity I get to play my role in cultivating pipeline for future leaders. Having my fingerprints on their leadership path will remain the most gratifying part of my professional life. Giving in life is always more luxuriating than getting in life. A leader who does not give back is a leader incomplete.

You can spend a good part of your life becoming a leader. Once you become a leader, you may not and should not rest. You may have achieved your objective, but the ambitious inner soul will push you to do more. Your goal is still not achieved until you leave that legacy. To leave the legacy, you need to define the legacy you want to leave. That is your goal! Timing is of essence in the leadership life cycle. Great leaders can hear the crescendo clearly and exit with a standing ovation at the right time. They know they have just authored the renaissance. The leadership lexicon is accomplished.

Leadership is not a destination; leaving a meaningful impact is.

Being a great leader should not be one of your goals; it should be your *only* goal. If you fail, you might end up as a good leader.

Ignorance is an incessant sea. Let learning be the life raft.

Thank you for taking the time to read my book.

APPENDIX

HOW TO MAKE THIS BOOK INTERACTIVE FOR YOUR STUDENTS

To make this book as interactive as possible for undergraduate and graduate students, and to engage students with different learning styles, I recommend that instructors incorporate a wide variety of interactive features into the curriculum associated with this book project. Here are just five examples:

1. Watch and discuss the brief video clips from interviews with Fortune 500 company CEOs on my company website at www.gdmus.com.
2. Embed this book in PowerPoint-based instruction using the "Interaction" feature.
3. Add media-rich interactions to your course by moving your content away from PowerPoint and into iSpring Visuals.
4. Use platforms such as Book Creator to combine text, images, audio, and video to create interactive stories, case studies, digital portfolios, and exercises.
5. Invite the author to your class for a live or virtual discussion with the students. Subject to author's availability.

GLOSSARY

Asynchronous learning: A student-centered teaching method that is used often in online learning.

DEI: Diversity, equity, and inclusion

DEIA: Diversity, inclusion, equity, and access

Diversity: The differences among us that make us unique. Diversity is a fact; it is what we *are.*

Equity: A fair opportunity for all, according to each person's need. It requires effort for leaders to create equity in their organization by neutralizing barriers.

Inclusion: An effort to value others through meaningful engagement. It is a choice.

Integrity: Firm adherence to a code of moral values.

Intuition: The power or faculty of attaining to direct knowledge or cognition without evident rational thought and inference.

Leadership: The art of seeing things other people cannot see, creating a team composed of talented people, and then getting out of their way to let them achieve the vision.

Resilience: The ability to recover from or adjust easily to misfortune or change.

Servant leadership: The idea that a leader's job is to help his or her team succeed.

Synchronous learning: All types of learning in which both instructors and students are in the same place, at the same time.

INDEX

A

B

C

D

E

F

G

H

I

J

K

L

M

N

O

P

R

S

T

U

V

W

X

Y

Z

NOTES

NOTES

NOTES

NOTES

NOTES

NOTES

NOTES

NOTES